IELTS Advantage

Reading Skills

Jeremy Taylor
Jon Wright

DELTA PUBLISHING

DELTA Publishing
Quince Cottage
Hoe Lane
Peaslake
Surrey GU5 9SW
England

www.deltapublishing.co.uk

First published 2012

Edited by Catriona Watson-Brown
Designed by Caroline Johnston
Illustration on page 119 by Kathy Baxendale
Images by iStock (pages 7 (all), 19 (top left, centre, top right, bottom right), 31 (top, bottom left), 45, 81 (all), 93 (all), 117 (a, b, c)); Shutterstock (pages 19 (bottom left), 31 (bottom right), 97 Steve Mann/Shutterstock.com, 105 (2) Stanislaw Tokarski/ Shutterstock.com, 117 (d) Chris Hellyar/Shutterstock.com); Thinkstock (pages 57 (all), 69 (all), 105 (1, 3, 4, 5, 6), 117 (e)); and Cartoonstock (page 115)
Cover design by Peter Bushell
Printed in China by RR Donnelley

ISBN Book 978-1-905085-63-7

Author acknowledgements
We would like to thank our friends and family for their support while we were writing this book, in particular to Jon Marks for his help with the project. From Jon there's also a special thanks to Dawn for her love and patience.

Text acknowledgements
We are grateful to the following for permission to reproduce copyright material:
Food and Agriculture Organization of the United Nations for an extract from FAO Food and Nutrition Technical Report Series. Human energy requirements. Report of a Joint FAO/WHO/UNU Expert Consultation, Rome, 17–24 October 2001, p. 7. Reproduced with permission; Natural Gas Supply Association for an extract from 'Natural Gas in the Transportation Sector', www.naturalgas.org, copyright © Natural Gas Supply Association; The Telegraph for an extract adapted from 'How can we measure happiness?', 16 November 2010, www.telegraph.co.uk, copyright © Telegraph, 2010; Ingenious Britain, Inteligis Group for an extract from *Ingenious Britain* newsletter, 26 February 2012, p. 28. Reproduced with permission; Tribune Media Services for an extract from 'Bye bye banknote The End of Money', 27 February 2012, www.newscientist.com, copyright © 2012 Reed Business Information – UK. All rights reserved. Distributed by Tribune Media Services; Tribune Media Services International for an extract from 'Foiling the cheats in a world of high-tech trust' 27 February 2012, www.newscientist.com, copyright © 2012 Reed Business Information – UK. All rights reserved. Distributed by Tribune Media Services; The Telegraph for an extract from 'We need to recalibrate what we think of as success', 7 April 2012, www.telegraph.co.uk, copyright © Telegraph, 2012; Tribune Media Services International for an extract adapted from 'Social networks: Getting connected', 30 April 2012, www.newscientist.com, copyright © 2012 Reed Business Information – UK. All rights reserved. Distributed by Tribune Media Services; ABC Science Online for an extract from 'What is multi-tasking?', www.multitaskingtest.net.au/ the-science/what-is-multi-tasking copyright © ABC Science Online, www.abc.net.au/science; The Telegraph for an extract adapted from 'How the battle for Britain's technological future can be won on the playing fields of Eton (and every other school)', 11 January 2012, www.telegraph.co.uk, copyright © Telegraph, 2012; PsyBlog for an extract from '10 Ways Our Minds Warp Time, 8 June 2011, www.spring.org.uk. Reproduced with permission; and House of Lords for an extract from the *Immigration and Asylum Bill*, Schedule 13, Consequential Amendments, 3B, Parliamentary copyright © 1999.

In some instances, we have been unable to trace the owners of copyright material and we would appreciate any information that would enable us to do so.

Contents

Introduction

Who is this book for?

This book is for students who are planning to take the IELTS Academic Reading Test and who are aiming for a score of 6.5–7.0 or higher. Students who are taking the General IELTS Test can also benefit from the book, though it is aimed in particular at those taking the Academic Test. While the reading texts in this book, and those in the test, are broadly of an academic nature, they are not highly specialized. As with the test itself, you will not be expected to have specialist knowledge of the subjects discussed. This book contains many hours of work for the motivated student and offers intensive practice for everyone who wants to brush up their skills before taking the test.

How is it organized?

The book is divided into ten units based on topics commonly found in the IELTS Reading Paper. Each unit is divided into different sections so that you can:

- get to know the many question types that may appear in the IELTS Reading Paper
- develop reading skills which will help you cope with the large amount of reading required in the test
- learn strategies which will help you make effective use of your time when taking the exam
- broaden your vocabulary, with particular attention paid to paraphrases, synonyms and collocations, which are all essential for students who want to get a good result in the IELTS test.

At the back of the book, you will find useful pages that will help you become more confident with some of the essential skills you need to be successful at IELTS, such as suggested websites that will give you hours of useful reading practice, tips for effective vocabulary learning, problems to avoid when filling in the answer sheet and how to get the most from your dictionary.

How can it help me get a better IELTS score?

Many students do not do well on the IELTS Reading Paper, not because their English is poor, but because they lack the strategies that will help them get a good result. This book will teach you a range of strategies for reading more effectively and for understanding the text more easily, and give you a lot of guidance about the best way of how to approach the various question forms. Some of the texts are slightly longer and harder than those you will find in the test – stretching you a little so that there should be no nasty surprises when you come to the test itself.

In addition to reading and completing the exercises in the book, we recommend that you:

- add useful new vocabulary to a separate notebook. While you will not be expected to have any specialized vocabulary for the test, the broader your vocabulary in English, the easier the Reading Paper will be for you
- underline phrases and collocations throughout this book, as these are the building blocks of a text. Then decide if they are worth writing in your notebook and learning
- time yourself while you read some of the texts and compare your times with your colleagues. Being able to read quickly is a very useful asset in the IELTS Reading Paper
- make contact with other IELTS students online and support each other in your studies, especially if you do not have the benefit of studying with other students in a classroom
- read, read, read. The more you read, the easier and more enjoyable it becomes. In this book, we give recommendations for the kinds of material you may find useful. With the Internet, there are many opportunities for the well-motivated student to get extra reading practice.

Can I use the book for self-study?

Yes, you can. The book works well for classroom use and also for self-study. In class, you have the benefit of discussing the questions with your classmates, while at home you have some peace and quiet to concentrate (we hope!); you also have the answer key and many comments to guide you through the answers. Discussion tasks are obviously easier when you are in a group. However, if you are studying on your own, we suggest you try this approach:

1 Make a list of your own ideas on the topic.
2 Put yourself in the position of someone who disagrees with you and make a list of the ideas they could have which are different from yours. To help you, imagine what these people would say:
   a someone 30 years older than you
   b someone who lives on the opposite side of the world to you
   c someone whose religious and political beliefs are different from yours
   d someone who has much more/less money than you do.
3 Imagine a dialogue between people with these different views: how would each person put forward and defend their arguments? How would they argue against opposing points?

Useful information about the IELTS Reading Paper

- You will take the Reading Paper **after** the Listening Paper and **before** the Writing Paper.
- Do not bring a mobile phone or any other communication device into the examination room. Just bring some pencils, an eraser and your ID.
- You will be given a reading text booklet and an answer sheet.
- The Reading Paper consists of three reading texts of approximately 900 words each, with the first text a little easier than the others.
- Each text is accompanied by 13 or 14 questions, with usually three or four different question types for each text. There are 40 questions in total, with 1 mark for each question.
- The test lasts for one hour; you do **not** have extra time to transfer your answers to the answer sheet. Aim to spend 20 minutes on each text, including writing your answers.

The IELTS Reading Paper

There are three reading passages in the test, with a total of 2,000–2,700 words (Academic Training) or 2,000–2,500 words (General Training). There are 40 questions, and you have one hour to do everything. There is no time at the end for you to transfer your answers to the mark sheet. That's why it is important to be able to read quickly and effectively.

The texts in the **Academic Training** module are taken from magazines, journals, books and newspapers. They are written for an educated but non-specialist audience. They are intended to be interesting and accessible to students who aim to enter university at undergraduate or postgraduate level, or for people intending to use English in their professional life. At least one of the texts will have a detailed logical argument that you have to follow. One text may include visual materials such as diagrams, charts or graphs.

In the **General Training** module, texts are taken from sources such as notices, advertisements, official documents, instruction manuals, leaflets and timetables, as well as books and magazines. The first section focuses on social survival. The second section focuses on training survival. The final section is general reading.

For both the **Academic** and **General Training** modules, the texts become progressively longer and more complicated, so it is a good idea to try to do the first section more quickly than the others.

There are a number of techniques and strategies you can use to read faster and understand more. In each unit of this book, we will give you practice with different types of exam question, and help you to improve your reading skills with some useful techniques.

Use this test to assess your current reading skills.

Are you a good reader?

1 How many hours do you spend reading in English in a normal week?
a) 0–1 b) 2–3 c) 4–6 d) 6–8 e) 9+

2 On average, how long do you spend reading each time?
a) up to 10 minutes b) 10–30 minutes c) 30–45 minutes d) 45–60 minutes e) more than 60 minutes

3 Tick which of these you have read **in English** in the past week:

A a timetable ❑ magazine ❑ a publicity poster ❑
a price list ❑ a telephone directory ❑
product information on food ❑

B an email from a friend ❑ a recipe ❑
a travel brochure ❑ a dictionary ❑
an advert or leaflet for a product or service ❑

C a review ❑ a blog ❑ an encyclopaedic entry ❑
a manual or set of instructions ❑
the lyrics to a song ❑ the blurb of a book ❑

D a whole newspaper or a short story or part of a novel ❑ a poem ❑ an academic text ❑
a semi-specialized article on a topic of interest ❑

Check your score

1 a) 0 b) 1 c) 2 d) 3 e) 4

2 a) 0 b) 1 c) 2 d) 3 e) 4

3 1 point for each answer in A;
2 points for each answer in B;
3 points for each answer in C;
4 points for each answer in D
In addition, give yourself 1 point for each full month between now and when you plan to take the IELTS test.

Results

0–10: You need much more practice to give yourself the best chance of getting a good score in IELTS.

11–15: You do read in English, but are not getting enough practice with reading different sorts of texts. You need to increase your focus on reading.

16–20: You are on the right track for getting a good result in IELTS. Try to increase the amount you are reading, and include a little more variety in your reading.

21+: Excellent! You give yourself a lot of reading practice. With a little more focus, you can get a great score in IELTS.

UNIT 1 Full of energy

In this unit, you will:

- discuss a range of energy sources and their effect on the environment
- study and practise **multiple-choice questions**
- study and practise **paragraph-heading questions**.

Getting started

1 Look at these three forms of energy production and discuss the questions below.

1 Are any of these systems used to produce energy in your country?
2 Which system is the best/worst for the environment?
3 Which system(s) do you think will still be in use in 100 years' time?

2 a Put these energy sources into the appropriate column of the table below.

biofuel biomass coal ethanol fossil fuel gas hydro-electric power nuclear power peat solar power tidal energy wind power

non-renewable energy resources	renewable energy resources

b Answer these questions about the energy sources.

1 Which of them involve burning?
2 Which do you think are the safest?
3 How many did you have to look up in a dictionary?

3 Discuss these questions.

1 What can we do to prepare for the time when non-renewable energy resources run out?
2 What effect does our thirst for energy have on the environment, and how is this likely to change in the future?

Spotlight on language

Energy collocations

1 Write four or five sentences that reflect your opinion or the situation in your country. Use these collocations, which are all based on the words *source* and *energy*, and the sentence beginnings below.

source of ... useful source of ... source material government sources
source of confusion source of information at source energy drink
green energy put your creative energies into ... solar energy energy loss

1 According to ...
2 The source of energy we read about most in my country ...
3 In my opinion, we should use more ...
4 Green energy is ...
5 A useful source of ...

Example: According to government sources, plans to promote green energy are now receiving more attention than ever before.

Collocations are an important part of natural, fluent language. You can be sure every text in the IELTS test will contain a number of them, as they are a frequent feature of all speaking and writing. Learning common collocations is also an excellent way to make your English sound more natural.
Write out collocations and useful expressions for different energy sources in your notebook – the more context you can give your examples, the better.

Working from context

2 Which energy sources are being talked about in these sentences? It is the same source in a, b and c in each case.

1 a As the seams of .... and iron were exhausted, or became unprofitable to work, mining and smelting diminished.
b After a leisurely tea by a .... fire, I asked the clerk to phone for a taxi.
c He watched Peter climb onto the large heap of .... by the wall and start to fill a bag.
Energy source = ...

2 a In the Philippines, the aim is to reduce the heavy dependence on imported ....
b I think it is fair to say that the really top-quality olives are usually sold in .... rather than in brine.
c In 2010, the tragedy at the Deepwater Horizon drilling rig led to the release of an estimated 750,000 cubic metres of .... into the sea, with serious ecological consequences.
Energy source = ...

3 a The question of how to create an economical and reliable supply of electricity without the costs and environmental disadvantages of .... power was approached from two separate directions.
b The Oxford Survey of Childhood Cancers compared the job histories of the fathers of children with cancers to those of the fathers of healthy children and found that those who worked with .... materials were more at risk.
c It is becoming increasingly difficult to take seriously claims that the civil side of .... power has nothing to do with .... weapons.
Energy source = ...

Spotlight on exam skills 1

Multiple choice

Multiple-choice questions test your ability to read for specific information. There are different types of multiple choice. This type offers you a 'stem' – sometimes an incomplete statement or a question – and three or four possible answers. Read the questions before you read the passage so you know what you are looking for.

1 Read this text, then answer the question that follows.

Tips

- You will not be penalized for wrong answers, so even if you don't know the answer, write something down.
- The different options for the answers include plausible 'distractors' – the wrong answers that only close reading will show to be wrong. These often contain key words from the text, so read carefully!
- You will not be expected to have any specialist knowledge of the subject.
- Read the question and options before you read the text and try to predict the answer.

Energy profile of the Czech Republic

The Czech Republic's dependence on energy imports has been quite favourable to date (32% of energy demand is met by imports); however, it is structurally unbalanced. The country's dependence on oil is about 95%, and in the case of natural gas, it is about 98%. The Czech Republic also imports nuclear power, but the primary resource, uranium ore, is available and produced domestically. In 2006, some 260,000 tonnes of oil and 150 mcm* of natural gas came from indigenous resources. However, the country's dependence on energy imports is expected to grow (to almost 50% by 2020). A number of direct and indirect measures must be adopted to slow the rate at which the Czech Republic's dependence on energy imports is increasing. Key measures include those geared towards promoting energy efficiency, supporting renewable energy resources in areas where they are effective (in accordance with the government's energy policy: 8% by 2010 and 16.9% by 2030), supporting nuclear energy (zero-emission energy sources) and improving the availability and extending the life span of the hidden potential of indigenous solid fuels, mainly brown coal.

*mcm = million cubic metres

adapted from www.euracoal.org

Which of these statements best describes energy use in the Czech Republic?

A The country imports almost all of its energy.

B The country's need for imported energy is likely to decrease through energy efficiency.

C The country considers nuclear power as one of the potential solutions to the problem of imported energy.

D The country aims to double its energy efficiency between 2010 and 2030.

Comments

A Not true: *... but the primary resource, uranium ore, is available and produced domestically.*

B Not true: Although energy efficiency is mentioned, it will not be enough to stop the Czech Republic's increasing need for energy imports.

C True

D Not true: The figures for energy efficiency are not given.

2 You are going to read a longer text about our increasing need for energy. Before you read, predict which of these topics are likely to be discussed.

energy-saving measures   nuclear power   pollution   health risks
population growth   scientific research   transport   finance

3 Read the text on page 10 and answer the three multiple-choice questions that follow.

Energy crisis? What crisis?

Looking at the forecasts for the world's energy demands for the future is pretty frightening. As the population of the world has increased, so has our thirst for energy. Should we build more nuclear power stations, as these don't produce the carbon dioxide that conventional coal or gas-fired power stations produce? But wait a minute – nuclear power is dangerous! Following the accident in Cernobyl in 1984, many people turned against nuclear power, preferring greener options like wind and solar power. But how reliable is wind power? Even in windy parts of the world, like western England, the wind turbines are not always turning. What could make up the shortfall when the wind stops blowing? Coal? Far too dirty. Gas? Cleaner than coal, but it still produces carbon dioxide. Nuclear? Too dangerous and politically sensitive. Solar power? In northern Europe? You must be joking.

That future generations will have to find alternatives goes without saying. Without trying to sound too apocalyptic, there is no way that we can maintain our present lifestyles. It is still not clear just how much damage we have already done, and are currently doing, to the planet, but the vast majority of scientists believe that we have to do something.

If we accept that change has to take place, we can consider what the catalyst will be for such change. Will it be governments telling us to save energy in various ways? Will it be companies producing ever more energy-efficient products? Or will it be people that change? Some may change for ideological reasons, believing that to save the planet they will need to change and will stop driving their gas-guzzling four-by-fours and heating their houses to 25 degrees in winter so that they can sit in shorts and a T-shirt to watch their home cinema. Many more are likely to change, not for ideological reasons, but for financial ones. As the price of energy increases – which, unless a new cheap source of energy is found, it almost certainly will – people will face stark choices; money for food or money for heating. (Interestingly, since the recent financial crisis, there has been a significant increase in the number of people growing their own food and consequently the demand for allotments, once seen as the preserve of old men, has skyrocketed.)

It is quite probable that we won't be able to rely on the governments of the world to get us out of this difficult situation. Most democratic governments are not around for more than a decade, so it is clear that they are more likely to look at the short-term rather than long-term difficulties.

Perhaps surprisingly, some of the poorest people in the world will be least affected. If you are a subsistence farmer, growing enough food for your family and just a few more vegetables to sell at the market, then you are unlikely to have high energy requirements. However, if you can't live without your car and spend a high proportion of your income on energy in its various forms, then it is highly likely that you will have to accept some quite dramatic changes in your life.

1 According to the writer, our energy needs in the future …
- **A** will depend on how the climate changes.
- **B** involve equally dangerous options.
- **C** have no easy solution.
- **D** must include a cleaner use of gas.

2 The writer feels that most people will change their behaviour ...
- **A** because energy will be more expensive in the future.
- **B** because governments will encourage a change in attitude.
- **C** because new technology will improve energy efficiency.
- **D** for ideological reasons.

3 According to the text, in recent times demand for allotments has ...
- **A** fallen quickly.
- **B** steadily declined.
- **C** risen slowly.
- **D** increased dramatically.

Comments

1 The answers to the questions are in order in the text, so you can presume that the answer to number 1 is somewhere near the beginning.
- **A** Not correct. Aspects of climate are mentioned, but not climate change.
- **B** Not correct. Danger is only mentioned in connection with nuclear power.
- **C** Correct. The fact there are questions about each form shows there is no easy answer.
- **D** Not correct. Gas is mentioned, but not as a 'must'.

2 The key to the answer is in the words *most* in the question and *many more* in the key sentence in the text.
- **A** Correct
- **B** Not correct: This is speculative.
- **C** Not correct: This is also speculative.
- **D** Not correct: More will change for financial reasons.

3 You may well not know the word *allotment*, but you don't need to know it to be able to answer the question. The text states that *there has been a significant increase in the number of people growing their own food and consequently the demand for allotments … has skyrocketed*. Again, you may not have seen the word *skyrocketed* before, but the word does suggest something going up very quickly, so the answer is D.

Vocabulary builder 1

Building your bank of words and phrases

As you work through this book, you will increase your vocabulary in the process. This will help you read faster and understand texts more easily. Keep a notebook with you and add any useful new words, expressions or collocations to it, ideally with a bit of context so that you can see how the word or phrase is used. One very important focus is on developing your awareness of paraphrase – different ways of saying the same thing. This is because in the test, the questions will rarely use the same grammar and key words as occur in the text.

1 Look at the relevant paragraphs of the text on page 10 and find words or expressions that have a similar meaning to these definitions.

1 quite scary (paragraph 1) pretty frightening
2 normal, traditional (paragraph 1)
3 more environmentally friendly (paragraph 1)
4 compensate for a deficiency (paragraph 1)
5 is obvious (paragraph 2)
6 continue living as we do (paragraph 2)
7 types of car that consume a lot of fuel (paragraph 3)
8 have difficult decisions to make (paragraph 3)
9 solve this problem (paragraph 4)
10 use most of the money that you earn to buy something (paragraph 5)

2 Which of the words or expressions in Exercise 1 do you think will be most useful for you?

Spotlight on exam skills 2

Paragraph headings

To match paragraph headings to paragraphs, you have to understand the basic idea – the 'gist' – of a paragraph. There will always be more headings than you need.

Tips
1 Read the headings before you read the text so you know what to focus on.
2 Check the instructions to see if you can use a heading more than once.
3 Identify key words in the headings.
4 Scan the text for similar ideas and paraphrases of key words.
5 Remember that the first paragraph of a text is often a general introduction to the topic, so see if one of the headings seems more general than the others.
6 When you have matched a heading and a paragraph, cross out the heading.
7 Check your answers by re-reading the paragraph and ensuring the heading is a logical summary.

1 Which of these is the best title for the passage on page 12?

A
Solar power turns darkness to light in Zimbabwe

B
Ambitious project curtails land degradation

C
UNDP invests $7 million in Zimbabwe

D
Shamva's farmers share solar power systems

In the early 1990s, numerous villages turned to solar power in parts of Africa where one might least expect to stumble upon an oasis of lights shimmering in the pitch-black night. Perhaps the most ambitious project of this nature, and one that is often cited, is a Zimbabwean project supported by UNDP through the Global Environment Facility (GEF). The initiative, jointly funded by GEF ($7m) and Zimbabwe ($400,000), installed some 9,000 solar power systems throughout the country in a bid to improve living standards, but also to curtail land degradation and pollution.

The River Estate near Shamva, 70 kilometres from Zimbabwe's capital, Harare, boasts one of the best solar-village models in the country. Fifty-two commercial farming families share systems; there is one system for every two houses. Each family has two lamps and a connection for a radio or small television set. The new lighting systems have improved the quality of life for the community. They have extended study hours for schoolchildren, reduced rural-to-urban migration in the area, and upgraded health standards by electrifying a local health centre.

adapted from www.un.org

Comments
Although B, C and D all mention things from the text, it is only A which encompasses the information from the whole text, so A is the correct answer.

2 Read the paragraph below and decide which of these headings best suits it, and why.

A A difficult balancing act for news organizations
B The potential dangers of alternative medicine
C Alternative medicine fights back

Many news organizations are desperate to be seen as being fair to all sides. For example, when a doctor is on a news programme to talk about the potential dangers of alternative medicine, there will almost certainly be an alternative-medicine practitioner on the same programme. The presenter of the programme, keen to remain neutral, gives them both equal air time to put their side of the story. But does this give a realistic view to the public? Perhaps by remaining neutral, the news organizations are giving an unbalanced view.

Comments
While alternative medicine is mentioned in the paragraph, it was only used as an example to illustrate a wider problem: the difficulty that news organizations face is trying to present the facts and remain neutral at the same time. Therefore A is the answer.

3 Read the text *Our energy requirements* on page 13. It has seven paragraphs, A–G. Choose the correct heading for each paragraph from the list above the text. There are more headings than you need. Write the correct number (i–x) next to each question (1–7).

1 Paragraph A ......viii......
2 Paragraph B ....
3 Paragraph C ....
4 Paragraph D ....
5 Paragraph E ....
6 Paragraph F ....
7 Paragraph G ....

List of Headings

- i The process of physical development
- ii Dealing with food
- iii Beneficial activities
- iv Reserves of fat
- v Mother's milk
- vi Forms of exertion
- vii Expecting a baby
- viii Essential processes
- ix Mental relaxation
- x Energy as a key to life

Our energy requirements

As human beings, we depend on energy in many ways.

A ....

This comprises a series of functions that are essential for life, such as cell function and replacement; the synthesis, secretion and metabolism of enzymes and hormones to transport proteins and other substances and molecules; the maintenance of body temperature; the uninterrupted work of cardiac and respiratory muscles; and brain function. The amount of energy used for basal metabolism in a period of time is called the *basal metabolic rate* (BMR), and is measured under standard conditions that include being awake in the supine position after ten to 12 hours of fasting and eight hours of physical rest, and being in a state of mental relaxation in an ambient environmental temperature that does not cause heat-generating or heat-dissipating processes. BMR represents 45 to 70 per cent of daily total energy expenditure and is determined mainly by the individual's age, gender, body size, body composition and lifestyle.

B ....

Eating requires energy for the ingestion and digestion of what we put in our mouths, and for the absorption, transport, interconversion, oxidation and deposition of nutrients. These metabolic processes increase heat production and oxygen consumption, and are known by terms such as *dietary-induced thermogenesis, specific dynamic action of food* and *thermic effect of feeding*. The metabolic response to nutrition increases total energy expenditure by about 10 per cent of the BMR over a 24-hour period in individuals eating a mixed diet.

C ....

This is the most variable and, after BMR, the second largest component of daily energy expenditure. Humans perform *obligatory* and *discretionary* physical activities. Obligatory activities can seldom be avoided within a given setting, and they are imposed on the individual by economic, cultural or societal demands. The term "obligatory" is more comprehensive than the term "occupational" that was used in the 1985 report (WHO, 1985) because, in addition to occupational work, obligatory activities include daily activities such as going to school, tending to the home and family and other demands made on children and adults by their economic, social and cultural environment.

D ....

Discretionary activities, although not socially or economically essential, are important for health, well-being and a good quality of life in general. They include the regular practice of physical activity for fitness and health; the performance of optional household tasks that may contribute to family comfort and well-being; and the engagement in individually and socially desirable activities for personal enjoyment, social interaction and community development.

E ....

The energy cost of growth has two components: 1) the energy needed to synthesize growing tissues; and 2) the energy deposited in those tissues. The energy cost of growth is about 35 per cent of total energy requirement during the first three months of age, falls rapidly to about 5 per cent at 12 months and about 3 per cent in the second year, remains at 1 to 2 per cent until mid-adolescence, and is negligible in the late teens.

F ....

During pregnancy, extra energy is needed for the growth of the foetus, placenta and various maternal tissues, such as in the uterus, breasts and fat stores, as well as for changes in maternal metabolism and the increase in maternal effort at rest and during physical activity.

G ....

The energy cost of lactation has two components: 1) the energy content of this food for the baby; and 2) the energy required in its production. Well-nourished lactating women can derive part of this additional requirement from body fat stores accumulated during pregnancy.

adapted from www.fao.org

4 Read this checklist and the related expert advice.

question	expert advice
1 Did you read the question carefully and write i–x in the right place?	*You must write i–x, not 1–10.*
2 Did you leave any answers blank?	*If you did, you're throwing away points. If you really don't know, guess.*
3 Did you start by reading the text slowly and carefully?	*This is not a good idea. The first time you read the text, you should read quickly to get the gist.*
4 Did you read the headings before or after you read the text?	*Most effective readers read the questions first, so they know what information they are looking for, then read the text.*
5 Did you read the text quickly to get a general idea of the content?	*This is a good strategy to use.*
6 Did you reread one paragraph at a time trying to find a suitable match?	*This is good. Focus on one paragraph, read all the headings, find the best match, then move on to the next paragraph.*
7 Did you reread the headings, then reread the whole text to find a match each time?	*This wastes your time because instead of rereading the headings, which are short, each time, you reread the whole text. Don't do this.*
8 Did you look for the same words in the heading and the paragraphs?	*Be careful. You might spot the same word in a heading and paragraph, but that doesn't mean the heading summarizes the key idea.*
9 Did you find words which have the same meanings as the headings in the paragraphs?	*Often the heading will summarize or paraphrase a paragraph.*
10 Did you cross out the headings as you used them?	*Do this – it saves time and makes it easier to match the remaining headings.*
11 Did you cross out the example heading already given before you matched the others?	*Again, this helps you save time.*
12 Did you look up any new words or expressions in the dictionary?	*In the test, you won't be able to use a dictionary. You should try to practise working out the meanings of new words from the context.*

5 You are going to read an article about using natural gas in cars. Before you read, predict which of these topics will occur in the article.

cost engine design family life pollution road safety taxis storage

6 Now read the article on pages 15–16 and check your answers to Exercise 5.

Natural gas in the transportation sector

Natural gas has long been considered an alternative fuel for the transportation sector. In fact, natural gas has been used to fuel vehicles since the 1930s!

According to the Natural Gas Vehicle Coalition, there are currently 150,000 Natural Gas Vehicles (NGVs) on the road in the United States today, and more than 5 million NGVs worldwide. In fact, the transportation sector accounts for 3 per cent of all natural gas used in the United States.

In recent years, technology has improved to allow for a proliferation of NGVs, particularly for fuel-intensive vehicle fleets, such as taxicabs and public buses. However, virtually all types of NGVs are either in production today for sale to the public or in development, from passenger cars, trucks, buses, vans, and even heavy-duty utility vehicles. Despite these advances, a number of disadvantages of NGVs prevent their mass production. Limited range, trunk space, higher initial cost, and lack of refuelling infrastructure pose impediments to the future spread of NGVs.

Most NGVs operate using compressed natural gas (CNG). This compressed gas is stored in similar fashion to a car's gasoline tank, attached to the rear, top, or undercarriage of the vehicle in a tube-shaped storage tank. A CNG tank can be filled in a similar manner, and in a similar amount of time, to a gasoline tank.

1 ....

There are many reasons why NGVs are increasing in abundance and popularity. New federal and state emissions laws require an improvement in vehicle emissions over the foreseeable future. For example, the state of California has some of the most stringent environmental standards, many of which are currently unattainable with conventionally fueled vehicles. Natural gas, being the cleanest-burning alternative transportation fuel available today, offers an opportunity to meet these stringent environmental emissions standards.

In addition, natural gas is very safe. Being lighter than air, in the event of an accident, natural gas simply dissipates into the air, instead of forming a dangerous, flammable pool on the ground like other liquid fuels. This also prevents the pollution of ground water in the event of a spill. Natural-gas fuel storage tanks on current NGVs are stronger and sturdier than gasoline tanks.

Natural gas is also an economical alternative to gasoline and other transportation fuels. Traditionally, NGVs have been around 30 per cent cheaper than gasoline vehicles to refuel, and in many cases the maintenance costs for NGVs are lower than traditional gasoline vehicles. In addition to being economical, many proponents of NGVs argue that a transportation sector more reliant on domestically abundant natural gas will decrease the US dependence on foreign oil—allowing for a more secure, safer energy supply for the country.

2 ....

One of the primary reasons for pursuing alternative-fueled vehicle technology is to decrease environmentally harmful emissions. It is estimated that vehicles on the road account for 60 per cent of carbon monoxide pollution, 29 per cent of hydrocarbon emissions, and 31 per cent of nitrogen oxide (NOx) emissions in the United States. All of these emissions released into the atmosphere contribute to smog pollution, and increase the levels of dangerous ground-level ozone. Vehicles also account for the emission of over half of all dangerous air pollutants, and around 30 per cent of total carbon emissions in the US, contributing to the presence of "greenhouse gases" in the atmosphere. The environmental effects of NGVs are much less detrimental than traditionally fueled vehicles.

NGVs are much cleaner burning than traditionally fueled vehicles due to the chemical composition of natural gas. While natural gas is primarily methane, gasoline and diesel fuels contain numerous other harmful compounds that are released into the environment through vehicle exhaust. While natural gas may emit small amounts of ethane, propane, and butane when used as a vehicular fuel, it does not emit many of the other, more harmful substances emitted by the combustion of gasoline or diesel. These compounds include volatile organic compounds, sulfur dioxide, and nitrogen oxides (which combine in the atmosphere to produce ground-level ozone), benzene, arsenic, nickel, and over 40 other substances classified as toxic by the EPA.

Dedicated NGVs also produce, on average, 70 per cent less carbon monoxide, 87 per cent less non-methane organic gas, and 87 per cent less NOx than traditional gasoline-powered vehicles.

3 ....

NGVs as they exist today are best suited for large fleets of vehicles that drive many miles a day. Taxicabs, transit and school buses, airport shuttles, construction vehicles, garbage trucks, delivery vehicles, and public-works vehicles are all well suited to natural-gas fueling. Because these vehicles are centrally maintained and fueled, it is economical and beneficial to convert to natural gas.

The primary impediments to the public proliferation of NGVs include the high initial cost, limited refueling infrastructure, and automobile performance characteristics. NGVs, despite being cheaper to refuel and maintain, are more expensive initially than their gasoline-powered counterparts. However, as the technology becomes more advanced, the cost of manufacturing these vehicles should drop, which may then be passed along to the consumers.

In terms of refueling infrastructure, there are currently around 1,500 natural-gas refueling stations in the US, over half of which are open to the public. Although this is a small fraction of the number of gasoline-fueling stations in the country, as environmental standards and government incentives for NGVs increase, supplying natural gas as a vehicular fuel will become increasingly common.

While driving range, storage space, and initial cost are currently preventing the mass production of dedicated NGVs (which in turn is preventing the expansion of public natural-gas fueling stations), it is expected that with improved technology, research, and infrastructure, the use of NGVs in non-fleet settings will increase in the future. NGVs present an exciting opportunity to reduce the damage of one of our most polluting sectors.

adapted from www.naturalgas.org

7 Choose the best heading for each of the sections in the article in Exercise 6 (1–3). There are two headings you will not need.

A The advantages of NGVs
B The need for change
C Reducing carbon-monoxide emissions
D Who uses NGVs?
E An expanding refueling infrastructure

8 Match the words or expressions from the article (1–9) with words or expressions that have a similar meaning (a–i).

1 proliferation
2 impediments
3 attached
4 foreseeable future
5 stringent standards
6 unattainable
7 in the event of
8 detrimental
9 primary

a harmful 8
b fixed 3
c barriers 2
d main 9
e great increase 1
f out of reach 6
g soon 4
h if this happens 7
i strict requirements 5

9 Find six more new expressions from the article that you think are useful and add them to your vocabulary book.

Note
You will never be asked to write a question like this in the exam, but writing one yourself will give you a much better understanding of the question form. It's also good reading practice.

Producing a paragraph-heading question

10 a Find a paragraph from a newspaper or magazine that has a heading. Now write three other headings for the paragraph.

b Show your paragraph-heading question to your colleagues. Can they work out which heading was the original one?

Vocabulary builder 2

Energy idioms

1 Match the idiomatic phrases in italics (1–7) with their meanings (a–g).

1 Robert's *a bright spark* – he'll know the capital of Mongolia.
2 Andrea's *full of beans* this morning.
3 Do you really think we can sell our cars in Japan? It's like *taking coal to Newcastle*.
4 After a tough day at work in the office, Ruth loves to *let off steam* with a game of squash.
5 There are six months before my IELTS test, so from now on, it's *full steam ahead*.
6 Steffi has been *burning the midnight oil* for the last two weeks.
7 Derek is already in a bad mood. Don't tell him about the broken photocopier right now. That will just be *adding fuel to the fire*.

a release (nervous) energy
b time to go at top speed
c has a lot of energy
d working late at night
e making a bad situation worse.
f an intelligent person
g supplying something where it is not needed

2 Do you have the same expressions in your language? Can you think of any others?

Modifiers and intensifiers

Modifiers and intensifiers are often used with adjectives to qualify the meaning of an expression in some way.
Looking at the forecasts for the world's energy demands for the future is ***pretty*** *frightening.*
As in the above example, they often serve to convey the opinion of the author.

3 These words occur in pairs including modifiers/intensifiers in the text on page 10. How many pairs can you remember? Now check the text to see if you were right.

highly almost certainly dangerous likely ever far more no probable quite too too way

Tip
It's a good idea to make a collection of phrases and expressions using modifiers and intensifiers as you read. Firstly, this is useful for practising reading in 'chunks' (see page 26). In addition, we use modifiers or intensifiers to qualify what we are writing or talking about, which can show our attitude towards something. In the IELTS test there are often questions that focus on the author's opinions.

4 Choose the best word to complete these sentences.

1 Working in a coal mine is a(n) *totally* / *extremely* dangerous job.
2 People who work on oil rigs are generally *so* / *very* well paid, but they do work *incredibly* / *definitely* hard.
3 Many people in Germany are *totally* / *ever* opposed to nuclear power.
4 Putting solar panels on the roof of your house is *wholly* / *relatively* easy.
5 If you live in a cool country and don't insulate your house properly, your energy bills are likely to be *extremely* / *absolutely* high.
6 I *certainly* / *quite* want to get a good grade in the IELTS test.

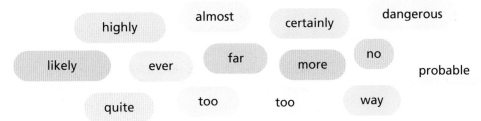

CLASSROOM WORKOUT

Defending one kind of energy supply

- Work in groups. Each group chooses a different fuel source and thinks of as many advantages of its chosen fuel source as possible in five minutes.
- Make notes – and try to include key words and expressions from the different texts in this unit.
- After the five minutes, take turns to stand up and tell the rest of the class the advantages that you came up with. Use your notes, but don't read from them. This will be followed by two minutes of questions from your fellow students, so be ready for some tricky questions.

CHECK YOURSELF

- Make a list of 10–15 collocations or expressions that you could use in a discussion on the topic of energy.
- Write down five facts you know about energy as a result of reading the texts in this unit.

SUMMARY

In this unit, you:

- discussed the range of energy sources available and their effect on the environment. What conclusions did you come to?
- looked at collocations connected with energy. How many have you written down in a notebook?
- studied and practised **multiple-choice questions**. What are the key things to remember about them?
- read about energy supply in the Czech Republic. Is the Czech Republic in a better or worse situation compared to your country?
- read about a potential energy crisis. Do think there will be an energy crisis, or will we be able to make a smooth transition to sustainable resources?
- started building up your bank of words, phrases and paraphrases. You should check back on your list regularly, adding new words whenever you can.
- studied **paragraph-heading questions** and practised them. Do you feel that you can cope with this kind of question in the test now?
- practised writing your own paragraph-heading questions. How difficult was it to create plausible distractors?

Over to you

1 Ask your friends how they feel about the world's energy resources.
2 Read newspapers and magazines to find out the latest news on energy issues and how they affect the world environmentally and politically.
3 What would you suggest to someone who asked for advice about how to reduce their energy consumption?

UNIT 2 Health, wealth and happiness

In this unit, you will:
- practise skimming, scanning and speed-reading techniques
- study and practise **sentence completion**
- read different types of text.

Getting started

1 These photos show important factors for staying healthy. Discuss the questions below.

1 To what extent is cost a factor in these things?
2 Which of these factors most often occur(s) in the news in your country? Why?

2 Rank these factors from 1 to 10 in terms of importance for your health (1 = most important).
- not smoking
- not drinking alcohol
- getting enough sleep
- avoiding stress
- eating healthy food
- keeping in touch with friends and family
- taking regular exercise
- avoiding exposure to the sun
- avoiding polluted areas
- getting immunised against preventable diseases

3 Discuss these questions.
1 Why do some people find it difficult to do the right thing for their health and well-being?
2 Do you think enough is done to promote campaigns for/against any of the factors in Exercise 2?
3 Which of these things should be controlled by the government, and which should be left to the individual?

Spotlight on language

Health and happiness collocations

1 Make as many collocations connected with health and happiness as you can by combining words and phrases from box A with those from box B.

A	B
chill	condition
cut down on	factor
feel-good	fiddle
fit as a	headache
on cloud	lifestyle
out of	modified starch
over the	moon
sedentary	nine
splitting	out
stop	smoking
be in high	spirits
watch	your weight

2 Complete these sentences with collocations from Exercise 1.

1 Victoria has been ...in high spirits... ever since she got into Cambridge University.
2 The diet magazine says that a good way to lose weight is to ....
3 When Petra got her exam results, she was .... She passed with flying colours.
4 I put in such long hours at work that when I get home I just ....
5 My grandfather's 93, but he's as ....
6 It is common for footballers to say they are .... when they are asked how they feel about winning a big match.
7 Our dependence on computers has meant that many of us lead a ....
8 That noise is giving me a ....
9 The single most important thing anyone can do to improve their health is ....
10 Physical exercise releases endorphins into your blood, and that gives you a ....
11 I can't have any chocolate. It's not an allergy – I'm just ....
12 I'm going to start jogging again because I'm ....

3 Discuss to what extent you agree with these comments, and explain why.

Health and happiness are connected. You can't be happy if you're not healthy.

You have to work at being healthy, but being happy is something you can't really control.

You can decide to be happy, whatever your circumstances.

Spotlight on exam skills 1

Skimming and scanning

While you can go into the IELTS test with a lot of confidence and even enthusiasm, one thing you don't have a lot of in the exam is time. Your ability to read quickly and to process the information effectively is of paramount importance. Each text that you have to read will be up to 900 words long, so you need to develop the ability to read quickly. Two key techniques that can help you do this are skimming and scanning.

Skimming strategies
Skimming involves running your eyes quickly over the text to find out the main ideas contained within it.
It is useful to:

- read the questions first to know what you are looking for
- read the title of the text and any subheadings
- read the first paragraph to see where the article is heading
- read the first line of each subsequent paragraph
- read the last paragraph, which may include a summary and/or conclusion
- see how any diagrams or pictures could relate to the article.

While skimming, you should:

- try to read three or four times faster than normal
- get a good idea of what the article is about without checking new words in the dictionary
- underline key words, e.g. dates, places, figures
- focus on key words like nouns, verbs, adjectives.

Scanning strategies
When you look for someone's name in a telephone directory or look a word up in a dictionary, you don't read every line. You can scan through the text to find the information that you are looking for. For this to be successful, you need to know what you are looking for. That means you should read the question first and identify key words in it to guide you.
It is useful to:

- read the questions so you know what you are looking for
- find the relevant part of the text as quickly as possible
- avoid reading the text line by line
- avoid mouthing the words as you read
- be aware of key words in the distractors that may also occur in the text. They may wrongly make you think you have the right part of the text.

While scanning, you should:

- look for key words in the text – nouns that reflect the questions, and words like *problem, solution, idea, goal, improvement, danger*
- look for key words that help you interpret the text and the writer's opinion – verbs like *must, can, help, ensure, increase, offer, measure, change* and adjectives and adverbials like *probably, without doubt, definitely, possible, much worse*
- think of paraphrases for key words from the question and look for them in the text.

The two strategies – skimming and scanning – work together. If you have skimmed the text effectively, then you will have a better idea of where to find the information you are looking for. You may have underlined an important fact, date, figure or key word. While scanning, you may notice other key words which you can underline.

Five ways to practise skimming and scanning

1. Get into the habit of reading longer texts and articles in English regularly.
2. Pay particular attention to the first and last paragraphs of an article.
3. To get the key ideas of a text, before you read, ask yourself: who, where, what, why, when and how? Try to find the answers to those questions as you read through an article.
4. Don't focus on new vocabulary, and don't use a dictionary on your first reading of a text.
5. Don't try to vocalize the text as you read – use your eyes, not your voice.

1 Practise your skimming and scanning with the article below about happiness. Read it quickly to find out what it says about the following:

1 sources of happiness
2 the relationship between happiness and politics
3 research into happiness
4 living standards and happiness
5 how to measure happiness
6 how different countries promote happiness

How can we measure happiness?

by Philip Johnston

Western leaders are looking beyond traditional indices of economic and social well-being and turning to ways of measuring national happiness.

What makes you happy? The smell of new-mown grass on a spring morning, perhaps; or the laughter of your children. For many of us, happiness is spiritual, individual, difficult to define and ephemeral. A Buddhist monk with no possessions beyond his clothes and an alms bowl might consider himself happier than a City financier with homes on three continents.

Personal happiness is something we all aspire to; so what about national happiness? Can the well-being of a country be measured? Is it possible to aggregate all those individual experiences into a happiness index that can be published quarterly, along with crime statistics, inflation rates and unemployment figures? Some political leaders think it is. They subscribe to the idea that measuring a nation's well-being by its economic output is a policy dead-end. Is this wise?

The consideration of happiness and how to maximise it is hardly a new activity. It has exercised great minds from Socrates to Montaigne and on to Bentham, Mill and the authors of the American Declaration of Independence. But while philosophers tended to deal with how we should lead our lives as individuals, the idea of happiness both as a science and a specific aim of national policy has only taken off in the past decade or so.

It is hardly surprising that the idea appeals to many politicians, especially when most of the economic news is gloomy and government policy is couched in the downbeat language of austerity. In such circumstances, looking beyond the traditional measurements of national well-being is a great temptation, even if it risks being criticized as a gimmick that has no place in the serious business of politics.

Moreover, economists believe that the pursuit of public happiness as a policy goal has merit even when the economy is booming. This is because, as their data have become more comprehensive and sophisticated, they have noticed one apparent paradox: that despite the fact that Gross Domestic Product (GDP) has increased substantially in the industrialized West, the levels of human contentment have remained static.

This realization encouraged Lord Layard, professor at the London School of Economics and adviser to a former prime minister, to urge the last

Labour government to recognize that economic growth need not be an overriding priority. He believed governments should embrace the principle that 'the best society is that where the people are happiest, and the best policy is the one that produces the greatest happiness'.

They found this hard to do because so little was known about what made people happy. But, as Lord Layard points out, 'The first thing we know is that in the past 50 years, average happiness has not increased at all in Britain or in the United States – despite massive increases in living standards.' In better-off countries, in other words, simply raising incomes does not make people any happier.

In truth, Prime Minister David Cameron has been thinking along these lines for a while. Shortly after he became Tory leader in 2005, he said: 'Well-being can't be measured by money or traded in markets. It's about the beauty of our surroundings, the quality of our culture and, above all, the strength of our relationships. Improving our society's sense of well-being is, I believe, the central political challenge of our times.' He added: 'It's time we admitted that there's more to life than money, and it's time we focused not just on GDP but on GWB – general well-being.'

In order to avoid a politically biased view of what constitutes national contentment, it would be essential to have an independent body such as the Office for National Statistics deciding what questions to ask and when to do so. A survey conducted in the middle of a cold, wet January, for instance, might produce significantly gloomier results than one carried out in summer months.

So what might a list of questions contain? Measurements of national well-being are already included in cross-border surveys carried out by the UN or the OECD* and include such indicators as a perceived lack of corruption; low unemployment; high levels of education and income; and the number of older people in the labour market. Using such criteria, polls can try to paint a picture of what a country thinks about itself.

It seems that modern politicians have bought so heavily into the idea that the state can do everything that they have deluded themselves into believing it can deliver the most elusive of all human desires: happiness. They have been persuaded that it is possible to measure life satisfaction and that its achievement on a national scale should be a goal of government. The difficulty is to establish an index that does not remain static or decline. After all, which politician will enjoy being accused of making his fellow citizens less happy than they were?

If measuring happiness is a relatively new phenomenon in the West, it has underpinned the public policy of one country for almost 40 years. The Kingdom of Bhutan has pursued the goal of 'gross national happiness' since 1972. In addition to the promotion of equitable socioeconomic development and the establishment of good governance, it also stresses the importance of the preservation and promotion of cultural values.

It probably helps, too, that there is little in the way of traffic, commuting into major cities does not involve an hour-long journey crushed together like sardines, television was banned until 1999 and the Himalayas provide a visual backdrop to a stunning sub-tropical landscape. No wonder they are happy.

* Organization for Economic Co-operation and Development

adapted from www.telegraph.co.uk

Sentence completion

1. Remember you're looking for specific information.
2. Do a grammar check as your read: does the gap require a singular or plural noun, a verb, an adjective, an adjective plus a noun …?
3. Use words from the text.
4. The stem is not likely to have the same words in the text, so skim the text for synonyms and paraphrases.
5. Be careful with spelling.
6. Remember that the answers are in the same order as in the text.
7. Numbers can be written as words or numbers (e.g. *ten* or *10*).
8. Hyphenated words count as one word (so *well-being* is one word).

2 Read the text on pages 22–23 again and complete these sentences with NO MORE THAN THREE words from the text. Use the scanning techniques on page 21 to help you find the answers. Underline the sections of the text that helped you to find the answers.

1. Some politicians feel that it is not wise to focus on a country's ....
2. Governments have only really taken the importance of promoting national happiness seriously in ....
3. While the idea of measuring happiness appeals to some politicians, others believe it could be .... for lacking in seriousness.
4. Although there have been .... in personal wealth, people in the rich West are not happier.
5. For David Cameron's government, the attempt to increase the .... of the people is a key priority.
6. Surveys may have different results depending on the weather, with .... results being possible for those carried out in winter.
7. As part of its policy of promoting happiness, the government of Bhutan thinks it is important to ensure the country remains true to its ....
8. According to the writer, Bhutan has the advantage of having almost no ...., which is a source of stress in Western countries.

3 When you have finished, answer these questions.

1. How long did you take on your first reading?
2. Which questions did you manage to answer?
3. Do you think you need more practice skimming and scanning?

Word building

One good way of building a large and flexible vocabulary is to focus on word building. For example, in the text on pages 22–23, a key word was *happiness*. Related words are *happy, unhappy, happier, happiest, unhappier, happily, unhappily*. Can you think of one more?

4 a Spend five minutes looking up the words related to *happy* in the dictionary to find expressions they occur in, then decide which is needed to complete each of these expressions.

1. .... married
2. more than .... to …
3. .... ending
4. .... families
5. keep them ....
6. many .... returns
7. lived .... ever after
8. .... for me, …
9. .... hour
10. .... is a good book.

b It's a good idea to do this with one or two key words for each text you read. Which other key words could you choose from the text?

Dealing with new words

It is likely that the texts in the IELTS test will contain vocabulary that you are unfamiliar with. However, don't panic because:

1 you are sure to know the vast majority of the words and expressions in each text
2 many of the new words or expressions will not be important
3 important words or phrases are likely to be guessable from the context they are in.

In the test, you won't be able to use a dictionary, so you need skills and strategies for dealing with new vocabulary. Some of the most useful include:

- working out the meaning from the context
- working out the meaning from the form and function of the word or expression
- ignoring the word or expression if you think it is not important.

5 Read the text on pages 22–23 again and highlight every word or expression you have not seen before. Then write them in the appropriate section of this table.

I have not seen this word or expression in English before, but it is very similar to a word in my language.	I have not seen this word or expression in English before, but I can work out its meaning from the context.
I have not seen this word or expression in English before and I can't work out its meaning from the context, but this does not affect my overall understanding of the text.	I have not seen this word or expression in English before, I can't work out its meaning from the context, and, as a result, I don't have an overall understanding of the text.

Vocabulary builder

Paraphrase practice

1 Find two-word phrases in the text on pages 22–23 which match these definitions.

1 recently cut grass.
2 someone who works in the money markets
3 figures showing the level of thefts, physical attacks, etc.
4 statistics showing how many people are out of work
5 an official strategy developed for a whole country by the leaders of that country
6 something that seems to be illogical
7 an organization which works separately from the government
8 all the people who are in work

2 Which of these phrases are most useful? Find five more expressions in the text that you think are worth learning.

Spotlight on exam skills 2

Speed reading

The problems of reading slowly:

- You might not finish all the texts.
- You create extra pressure for yourself.
- You probably waste lots of time on sections of the texts that are not relevant to the answers you need.
- Slow reading does not necessarily make you a more accurate reader.
- You will probably read less in preparation for the test.

Being able to read quickly and accurately gives you many advantages:

- You get the gist of the texts faster, so can orient yourself more quickly.
- You will be more confident that you can read all the texts.
- You will be more confident of having enough time to answer all the questions.
- You have more time to check your answers.
- When preparing for the exam, you can get more practice with a wide variety of texts on different topics.

1 Read this text, paying attention to the 'chunks' or groups of words between the / marks.

One useful technique / to increase your reading speed is this: / when you read a line of text, / which is typically 12–14 words, / don't let your eyes rest on each word. / This is a very inefficient way of reading. / Your brain should have no problem / coping with chunks of language, / four or five words at a time. / This means you will move your eyes / three times per line, not 14. / It does take practice, / but it is a skill you should develop / if you want to get a good result / in the IELTS test. / This type of reading is / much easier when you know collocations and phrases / because in essence you 'chunk' the text / into groups of words that go together.

Another technique you can use to improve your reading speed is to focus your eyes more or less down the middle of the paragraph you are reading. Your brain can actually notice and make sense of the words around your focus. At first, this can seem strange and might not be easy to do, but it gets easier with practice.

2 Try to read the text on the next page about the history of Manchester in no more than one minute by focusing on the words in bold. Then decide whether each of these statements is true (T) or false (F).

1 The text is about the geography of Manchester.
2 The text is factual rather than opinion-based.
3 Manchester was already an important population centre when the Romans arrived.
4 The population only started to grow with the Industrial Revolution.
5 Without cotton, the history of the city would have been different.
6 The only work available in Manchester was in the cotton mills.
7 Transport was an important element of the Industrial Revolution.
8 The attraction of the work available was it was well paid.
9 Families in Ireland sent their children to work in Manchester.
10 The city briefly changed its name as a result of its rapid growth.

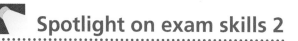

The History of Manchester

Although the history of **Manchester stretches back** to Roman times, when a small settlement grew up around the **Roman fort known as Mamuciam**, it was not until the later years of the eighteenth century that it became a **population centre** of any great magnitude. Records indicate the population grew from **10,000 to approaching** 80,000 in just a few decades, increasing to around 150,000 by **the Industrial Revolution**, which saw its transformation into the country's and the world's **leading industrial metropolis.**

The engine for this change was **cotton, which began to be** imported via the port of Liverpool and which was delivered **by canal to Manchester** in the latter part of the eighteenth century. The rapid and profitable **boom in textile manufacture** saw the streets of Manchester and surrounding towns become **home to huge numbers** of cotton mills, textile print works and engineering workshops. The **expansion of transport links** facilitated this development. In 1824, one of the world's **first public omnibus services** began in Manchester, quickly followed in 1830 by the **opening of the first steam passenger** railway linking Liverpool and Manchester.

Often overlooked, however, was the **'human fuel'** that made all this possible. The promise of work, however poor the pay, however **bad the conditions**, resulted in wave after wave of immigration from the surrounding **countryside and abroad**, the villages and towns of Ireland in particular, where terrible **poverty and the threat of famine** drove whole families to leave everything they knew for a life in **'Cottonopolis'**, as the city was dubbed.

Paraphrase practice

3 Decide if these expressions from the text above are similar in meaning to the expressions in italics or not.

1 of any great magnitude	*of some size and importance*
2 metropolis	*capital city*
3 the engine for this change	*what was mainly responsible for this development*
4 rapid ... boom in	*quick change in*
5 facilitated this	*made this possible*
6 often overlooked	*with a view over a particular place*

Identifying text types

We read different sorts of texts in different ways and for different purposes. For example, we don't read a telephone directory for pleasure, or try to learn facts from an advertisement. Being able to identify what sort of text you are reading helps you in many ways. Understanding the purpose of the text and knowing how the author expects you to react gives you control over how to read it more effectively.

4 Work in pairs. Discuss the differences between the types of text below. Think about:

- format and layout
- fact and opinion
- register and language
- grammar and vocabulary
- headings and illustrations
- length.

1 an advertisement / a history book
2 a legal document / a newspaper article
3 a personal story / a book review
4 an information leaflet / an encyclopaedia

Skimming for style

5 Read these extracts (A–H) from different types of text about immigration and match them to the text types in Exercise 4.

A

Immigration derives from the Latin word *migratio* and means the act of a foreigner entering a country in the aim of obtaining the right of permanent residence. Immigration may have economic or political motivation, or be a matter of family re-unification or caused by natural disaster. In many cases, immigrants simply desire to improve their circumstances by relocating.

B

Timofey Pnin is surely one of the most memorable of Nabokov's characters. We meet a bald and middle-aged teacher of Russian, and discover that he's completely lost. Much that he encounters in the world around him is a source of confusion, including timetables, the use of articles in English and also – comically – the habits of the Americans who are his neighbours. These are all things that many if not all fellow immigrants are likely to have in common with him. Yet Pnin is a unique character, both in life and in literature.

C

THE PRECISE date of the first human occupation of Australia is likely to remain unknown, but evidence has been uncovered to suggest human presence on the continent for at least 40,000 years. Migration from Europe dates from 1788, when the first transports bearing convicted criminals made the long journey south. This was quickly followed in the early 1790s by the first wave of voluntary – and hence free – immigrants.

D

Immigration control concerns both how and why people from countries outside the UK are allowed to enter the country and how long they are permitted to remain. Furthermore, it governs what they may and may not do while during their stay in the UK; for example, whether they have the right to obtain paid employment, whether relatives may join them here, and whether they have access to the National Health Service and similar state benefits. The paragraphs that follow give advice about all aspects of immigration control.

E

Syed Ahmed, 22, a bright and hard-working young man, is studying at a leading British university to become an accountant. When his application to renew his visa so he could stay here on completion of his three-year degree course was approved, the final decision was not based on the contribution he could make to this country. Instead, the fact he'd taken up playing cricket for a local club since his arrival from Bangladesh turned out to be the basis of the judge's decision.

F

With over 25 years' experience of providing a comprehensive range of immigration and legal services, we offer our clients a friendly and professional service for all immigration needs. Our extensive experience enables us to advise you on the prospects of success and problems to be aware of when submitting an application. Working together, we will use our experience to find a solution that matches your needs wherever possible. As specialists in business immigration, we have developed a range of strategies that can assist organizations in obtaining work permits, visas and rights to remain.

G

I came to this country at the age of 12. When I started high school, I could hardly understand the language. That seems an age ago. Now I'm married, studying at college and would like to become a teacher. Unfortunately, that can't happen as a result of my status as an illegal immigrant. The future now seems so uncertain. But we are good people, we don't have a criminal record, we pay taxes, we go to school, we work hard, and we love living here. I just want a chance to get the job I feel I deserve, and to normalize our situation. Ultimately, we aim to use the years we've been here as justification to become naturalized, so we can be treated as citizens of the country.

H

> If directions are given under Part I of Schedule 2 or Schedule 3 to the 1971 Act for a person's removal from the United Kingdom, and directions are also so given for the removal with him of persons belonging to his family, then if any of them appeals under section 59, 63, 66, 67 or 69(1) or (5), the appeal is to have the same effect under paragraphs 10 to 14 in relation to the directions given in respect of each of the others as it has in relation to the directions given in respect of the appellant.

Skimming for content

6 How many of the extracts in Exercise 5 mention:

1 education?
2 nationalities?
3 work?
4 free time?
5 law and law-breaking?

7 These expressions are taken from the extracts in Exercise 5, but each one has an extra word. Scan the extracts to find which one each expression is from and cross out the extra word.

1 speedy professional service
2 then quickly followed in
3 source of considerable confusion
4 entering a European country
5 all persons belonging to
6 have the legal right to
7 university degree course
8 hardly understand anything

Sentence completion

8 Answer these questions about the extracts in Exercise 5 using NO MORE THAN TWO WORDS for each answer.

1 The aspect of English grammar Pnin finds most problematic is ....
2 Preceding those who chose to settle in Australia by a few years, ... were the first European migrants.
3 Immigration control includes rulings on whether people are allowed to look for ....
4 The hope to live together again with one's .... is in some cases a reason for immigration.
5 The author of extract G hopes to change nationality by being .... as a result of the length of time she has spent in the country.
6 Extract H states that anyone under threat of .... from the country has a right to appeal.

9 Complete these sentences logically using the number of words indicated in brackets. Then compare your answers with a partner.

1 I spent last weekend .... *(2 words)*
2 I did/didn't go to the cinema last week because .... *(3 words)*
3 If I had more money, I would .... *(2 words)*
4 I feel happiest when I .... *(3 words)*
5 My favourite time of day is .... *(1 word)*
6 What worries me most about the future is .... *(3 words)*
7 Two techniques for reading quickly are .... *(3 words)*
8 All the short texts above involve the theme of .... *(1 word)*

CLASSROOM WORKOUT

Arguing a position

- Think about these two statements:
  – Health is far more important than happiness.
  – Happiness is far more important than health.
- Work in groups. Half the groups find as many arguments as possible which support the first statement. The other half do the same for the second statement.
- You have five minutes to think of your arguments. Try to use key expressions from this unit. Then present your argument to the class. The group with the most convincing arguments wins.

CHECK YOURSELF

- Make a list of five different sorts of text in English that you plan to read this week in order to practise skimming and scanning techniques. They must come from different sources and be on different topics. You should allow at least 20 minutes for each type of text.
- Make a list of 10–15 collocations or expressions that you could use in a discussion on the topic of health and happiness.
- Write down three facts you now know about ways of measuring happiness as a result of reading the texts in this unit.

SUMMARY

In this unit, you:

- looked at many words and collocations connected with health and happiness. How many did you write down in your notebook?
- read about skimming, scanning and speed-reading techniques. What are the advantages of reading quickly in the IELTS test?
- looked at **sentence-completion** questions. What common mistakes do some students make with this question type?
- looked at coping with new words. Do you know why it is not always necessary or useful to reach out for your dictionary when you come across unknown words?

Over to you

1 Look online to see what health issues are likely to become more important in the future.
2 Try to find three articles online or in newspapers and magazines about how to be happy and healthy.
3 Some people say that happiness is the by-product of doing something else. Think of three examples that prove or disprove this point and tell your friends.
4 Find some texts you think are interesting and practise breaking them into logical 'chunks'. If you work with a friend, see if you both agree on how to 'chunk' the same text.

UNIT 3 Communication

In this unit, you will:
- look at a range of communication methods and their related vocabulary
- study and practise **short-answer** questions
- study and practise more **multiple-choice** questions
- look at **pick-from-a-list** questions.

Getting started

1 Look at the three photos of ways of communicating. Where are/were they used? What are the advantages and disadvantages of each method?

1

2

3

2 Choose the four most important forms of communication from the list below for:

1 you, your friends and family
2 the world of business
3 the world of education
4 people who travel.

fax landline telephones email communication drums internet mobile phones letters face-to-face communication Morse code books newspapers posters radio public announcements social media

Justify your choices.

3 Discuss these points.

1 Give two reasons why people might choose not to use some of the means of communication listed in Exercise 2.
2 Which of the communication methods in Exercise 2 are likely to still be with us in the year 2100? Give reasons for your answer.

Vocabulary builder 1

Communication vocabulary

1 Match words from column A with words from column B, and words from column B with words from column C to form useful expressions about communication.

Examples: business communication, communication breakdown

A	B	C
business	communication	a message
channels of	communicator	breakdown
direct	communicative	door
effective	communicatively	effectively
global	communicate	in sign language
internal	communicating	problems
mass		skills
non-verbal		systems
online		
poor		
regular		
skilled		
successful		

2 Complete these sentences with expressions from Exercise 1.

1 Not speaking the same language as your customers can lead to communication breakdown.
2 One thing a(n) .... can do is to build trust with the other person.
3 The key to .... is to speak clearly and with a smile on your face.
4 It's imperative to have good .... when you work in sales.
5 All big companies invest massively in .... such as video-conference facilities.
6 I'm in .... with every member of my family.
7 According to social scientists, about 70% of our message is conveyed by ....
8 Even when relationships between countries are bad, it's important to keep .... open.
9 The ability to .... is important when you have deaf friends.
10 Letter writing has largely been replaced by ....

Working from context

3 Which forms of communication do these sentences relate to?

1 I only follow people that follow me, and I never open DMs from people I don't know.
2 You're through to Ms Grubshaw.
3 There seems to be a problem with the printing mechanism, so you'll have to send it away to be repaired.
4 Standing there with your hands in your pockets in an unironed shirt and shoes that have never known polish; what kind of impression do you think you're making?
5 -- --- ·-· ··· · -·-· --- -·· ·
6 I only recently found out that by holding down a key for longer, it makes the number appear rather than a letter.
7 Use more expensive paper and have your address and contact details printed at the top of the page if you want to make a professional impression.

Spotlight on exam skills 1

Short-answer questions

1 Read the questions (which follow the order of the text) and underline key words.
2 Scan the text, looking for the key words or synonyms and paraphrases.
3 Check the word limit required and stick to it!
4 Look at what structure (e.g. plural, verb form, prepositions) is required.
5 Make sure you copy words accurately.
6 You can write numbers as words or figures (*eleven* or *11*).
7 Hyphenated words count as one word.

1 Read this passage, then answer the questions below. Choose NO MORE THAN TWO WORDS from the passage for each answer.

Not just a lot of hot air

There is a revolution going on in Africa; not a political one, but an economic one. The driving force behind this revolution is the humble mobile phone. Once the preserve of the elite (which was also the case in Europe and America not so long ago), the mobile phone is now ubiquitous, as there are over 600 million African subscribers, from Morocco and Tunisia in the north to south Africa, with 93 million in Nigeria alone, putting it at the top of the list. However, others, like Egypt, are not far behind, and changes in sales taxes in Kenya, for example, resulted in a 200% increase of sales in one year. Even this figure does not truly reflect the number of users, as in rural areas it is common for many people to share a single phone, which explains why researchers claim that around 80% of Africans use mobile phones regularly.

Although many associate the continent principally with areas of business such as farming and mining, both of which do have a long and successful history there, we should not make the mistake of assuming that there is any less business innovation in Africa than in the industrialized nations. The banking industry has been quick to see the potential of increased phone use, and many Africans, notably in Kenya with 8.5 million users, now do their banking via a mobile phone.

1 What is the cause of the great change that is taking place throughout Africa?
2 Which social class has lost its monopoly of mobile phone use?
3 Where do most African mobile-phone users live?
4 Where are phones most likely to be co-owned?
5 Which area of business has taken most advantage of mobile phone usage?

2 Look at these answers to Exercise 1. Which of them are incorrect, and why? Make any corrections that are necessary.

1 mobil phone
2 the elite
3 in Nigeria alone
4 rural area
5 farming and mining

Comments
1 Incorrect: Check the spelling – the answer is *mobile phone*.
2 Correct
3 Incorrect: Check the word limit – the answer is *Nigeria* OR *in Nigeria*.
4 Incorrect: This should be plural – the answer is *rural areas*.
5 Incorrect: Answer is wrong (be careful when the question repeats key words from the text, as they are often distractors) and too long – should be *banking / banking industry*.

3 Answer these questions IN NO MORE THAN THREE WORDS.

1 What is the topic of the main story in today's news?
2 What has been the biggest surprise for you this week?
3 What do you most admire about your favourite person?
4 How would you improve the educational system of your country?
5 What's your main ambition for this year?

4 Find an interesting story in today's news. Make a list of questions that start:

- What ... ?
- Why ... ?
- How ... ?
- To what extent ... ?
- In which ... ?
- According to, ... ?
- Give a reason for ...

How many can you answer in three words or fewer?

Matching headings

5 You are going to read a passage called *Whale communication* on page 35. The text has six untitled paragraphs A–F. Choose the correct heading for each paragraph from the list of headings below (i–ix).

Questions 1–6

List of Headings

i Musical futures
ii Sad mystery to solve
iii Surprising discoveries
iv The inventiveness of song
v Singing effects
vi Threats to survival
vii Singing for supper
viii Varieties of song
ix The significance of song

1 Paragraph A ....
2 Paragraph B ....
3 Paragraph C ....
4 Paragraph D ....
5 Paragraph E ....
6 Paragraph F ....

6 Choose NO MORE THAN THREE WORDS from the passage for each answer.

Questions 7–12

7 What is the length of an individual whale song?
8 How far does a whale song carry?
9 What sound do whales emit in an effort to locate food?
10 What are whales in the same school believed to display through song?
11 What innovation enabled whales to be hunted in dramatically larger numbers?
12 What measures have been suggested to protect whales?

7 Find words or expressions in the passage which mean the same as the following.

1 nearly complete darkness (paragraph C)
2 a very short period of time (paragraph C)
3 especially (paragraph D)
4 have some function (paragraph D)
5 start a journey / have the intention of (paragraph E)
6 when two object strike each other with force (paragraph E)
7 impressive and inspiring (paragraph F)
8 suggest or indicate that (paragraph F)

Whale communication

A It is only comparatively recently that we have become aware of the hauntingly beautiful sounds made by humpback whales. The hydrophone, a microphone that can be used in water, was developed by the British scientist Ernest Rutherford, and is particularly good at detecting the presence of submarines underwater. During the Cold War, a Bermudian, Frank Watlington was working for the US government, and it was his job to use hydrophones to listen out for Russian submarines. While he was doing this, Watlington noticed that humpback whales appeared to 'sing'. Later, Watlington's work was taken up by two other researchers, Roger Payne and Scott McVay, who studied the nature of these humpback whale 'songs'. They found that the various sounds produced by the whale formed a song which lasts for about 30 minutes and is then repeated by the whale for hours or even days.

B Scientists believe there are two main reasons for whales to make sounds: echolocation, so that the whales know what objects (and perhaps food) are around them; and communication. Whales are capable of communicating to other whales over huge distances. Sound waves travel faster through water (around 1 kilometre per second) than through air, and the sound of a whale can travel thousands of kilometres through the oceans.

C Many different species of whale are capable of making noises and some of them (as well as dolphins and porpoises) are believed to use echolocation. Some whales look for food, such as squid, down to a depth of 1.5 kilometres, and at that depth there is virtually no light at all. Without being able to locate their food, the whales are going to go hungry. The whales send out series of clicks and listen out for the echo of the sound. From this, the whale is able to work out what is around it and can respond accordingly. The system whales use is highly complex, but it is similar to the way that you can tell direction of sound. You have two ears and when a sound is made, the sound reaches one ear a fraction of a second before the other. From this information, your brain can work out the direction of the sound.

D In addition to echolocation, some whales, most notably the humpback whale, are capable of producing a range of notes which appear to be a form of communication. Humpback whales in one school (as groups of whales are known) tend to sing virtually the same song. Perhaps like football supporters they are demonstrating group identity, showing that they belong to the same school. Other schools, particularly those found in other oceans, sing songs which are quite different. It is also quite likely that the songs play a role in courtship. It is generally the males that sing, so perhaps they are also trying to attract females.

E For millions of years, whales have swum in the great oceans of the world and only recently have they had to contend with a predator: man. In the 18th and 19th centuries, many countries had fleets of ships which set out to bring back whales. The 20th century saw the development of factory ships which were capable of killing and processing thousands of whales. In the 1930s, over 50,000 whales were killed annually. It wasn't until 1986 that a moratorium was agreed to stop whale hunting, and scientists hope that the number of whales will recover. So can the whales of the world now cruise about without a care in the world? Sadly not. The growth of trade in the world has meant that there are now more ships, particularly large container ships, than ever before. In fact, the Worldwide Fund for Nature (WWF) says that large numbers of northern right whales are killed in collision with ships. But it is not only the physical danger that ships present. The loud noises of ships' engines are very likely to disturb the whales, and the WWF have called for shipping restrictions in certain areas.

F In recent years, there have been many cases of whales dying on beaches. Could the reason for these tragedies have something to do with the noise pollution that these majestic creatures have to live with? There is no definite answer to the question, but it has attracted considerable research, and findings seem to point to man's industrial activities in the ocean. With an ever-growing need for oil, more and more drilling takes place offshore. To assess the likelihood of the presence of oil, seismologists use sonar to work out the underlying geology. The sounds used in such tests are believed by some people to have a highly damaging effect on whales, either simply disrupting their method of communication, or, some scientists believe, actually killing them. With an ever-increasing human population and dwindling resources, whales face an uncertain future. While it is unlikely that we will ever know exactly why whales producing their whale songs, the world will be a much poorer place without them.

Spotlight on language

Prefixes

Tip
When dealing with words you have not seen before, you can often work out their meaning from the context in which they appear and by breaking them up into component parts.

1 Look at these words taken from the article on page 35. Without looking back at the text, match the two parts of the word (1–3 to a–c), then match each word to its definition (i–iii).

1 kilo	**a** metre	**i** a vehicle which can operate underwater
2 hydro	**b** marine	**ii** an instrument which can be used to record sound in water
3 sub	**c** phone	**iii** a unit of distance equivalent to one thousand metres

2 Use a dictionary to find more words with these prefixes.

1 kilo- 2 hydro- 3 sub- 4 tele- 5 bi- 6 post- 7 pre-

Keep a list of new words with these prefixes in your notebook.

Spotlight on exam skills 2

Topic sentences

One good reason for paying particular attention to the first line of a paragraph is that this is normally the topic sentence. The function of a topic sentence is to express the main idea of the paragraph. This is essential guidance for the reader as to what the paragraph will be about.

Topic sentences generally consist of two parts: the topic itself and the controlling idea. You can think of the topic in terms of nouns or noun groups, e.g. life in the 20th century, the importance of social media, the communication of whales. These example topics are quite general, probably too general for the writer to tackle effectively.

The controlling idea is the specific focus on the topic the writer intends to develop. It usually reveals the writer's opinion or attitude towards the topic, or highlights a specific focus that defines, or limits, what the writer will write about. Consequently, it indicates the direction of the paragraph.

Look at this example:

The basics of any foreign language can be mastered *given sufficient time and practice.*

The topic is in bold, the controlling idea is in italics. It clearly states an opinion that defines and limits the topic. The reader would expect the rest of the text to deal with the time element and the sort of practice that will help you master a language.

1 Decide which are the topics, and which the controlling ideas, in these sentences.

1 People can overcome communication barriers by thinking carefully about the message they hope to impart.
2 There are several advantages to learning foreign languages at school.
3 Publicly available computer applications require little knowledge of programming skills for obvious reasons.
4 Newborn babies learn to become effective communicators quickly for a number of vital reasons.
5 Learning how to get what you want in business is not difficult if you follow these steps.
6 There are several ways to make a profit from starting your own blog.
7 Languages die out for a range of different reasons.
8 Successful advertising depends on specific features that capture the attention of the public.

2 Discuss whether you think these sentences follow on logically from the corresponding topic sentences in Exercise 1.

1 Failure to do this can result in anything from a simple misunderstanding between friends to causes of acute personal embarrassment and even lost business contracts worth millions of dollars.
2 As Latin has no native speakers, it is considered a dead language, which is why some argue that it is a waste of time to study it.
3 The various programming languages our technology depends on share many common features.
4 If they did not establish lines of communication with their carers, they would soon die, as they are incapable of feeding or protecting themselves from danger.
5 First, you must be very clear about what you want when you start any business transaction, and that in turn requires you to think about what your client wants from you.
6 Blogs have grown enormously in popularity in the past 18 months, and this is a trend that is set to continue.
7 Two interesting examples are gradual language death, which occurs when minority languages are in contact with a dominant language – as is the case with American Indian languages and English – and bottom-to-top language death, which is the process of the language beginning to change in places such as the home and the street until it only survives in special contexts such as religious services.
8 All advertising is an appeal to an audience to become a consumer of a given product or service of some sort.

Comments

1 Yes. It presents the consequences of failure to think carefully about intended messages.
2 No. It does not link with the controlling idea that there are advantages to learning languages.
3 No. It does not link to the controlling idea that the reasons are obvious.
4 Yes. It provides examples that explain why it is vital for babies to learn to communicate.
5 Yes. It is the first step mentioned in the controlling idea.
6 No. It is about blogs, but is not linked logically to the controlling idea, which is about ways of making money.
7 Yes. It cites examples of the different reasons language death can occur.
8 No. It doesn't link to the controlling idea, which makes the reader expect information on the specific features of advertising that capture the attention.

3 Read back through the texts you have read in the first three units of this book to find topic sentences and controlling ideas.

Be careful: not all types of text have topic sentences. Narratives, descriptions of processes and descriptive texts may not have topic sentences, as the development of ideas and arguments are perhaps not the main focus of these text types.

Word-building practice

4 Check in your dictionary to find expressions using these words and phrases.

1 .... a speech
2 speaking of ....
3 .... spoken
4 ....-speaking
5 on speaking ....
6 .... speaking
7 speak for ....
8 speaking as ....
9 .... speaker
10 on speaker ....
11 .... of speech

Multiple choice

1 Read the questions and underline the key words, which are usually nouns, names, verbs, dates, etc.
2 Scan the text and underline the key words and synonyms or paraphrases from the questions.
3 Be careful: if the same word(s) are in the option and in the text, it might be a distractor. Check the logic and meaning, not just the words.
4 Remember that the questions may focus on specific facts or opinions.
5 The final question may test your understanding of the text as a whole – its purpose or style, etc.
6 When you have identified the right place in the text, carefully analyze each option (A–D) one by one.

5 You are going to read a text about how languages change. Before you read, what do you think the text will say about the following?

1 animals
2 Latin
3 research into languages
4 language learning
5 age
6 culture

6 Read the text below to see if you were right.

Language is one of the defining characteristics of humans, and one of the key features that distinguishes humans from animals, so language loss raises serious questions about our history, our humanity and perhaps about our future, too. Any study of the history of language shows that languages, like humans, develop over time. According to some estimates, around 7,000 languages are still spoken in the world. This number is an indication of the diversity, vitality and range of human experience in all corners of the globe. But not all those languages are equally healthy. Continuing the metaphor of growth and development, while some languages are robust and powerful, others are in the process of disappearing. In fact, research indicates that languages are dying out at an unprecedented rate. Some believe that by 2100, the vast majority of these languages, perhaps as many as 90% of them, will no longer exist in the spoken medium. If this were plant life, or whales and dolphins, the outcry would be enormous. Yet, surprisingly, there seems to be little interest in this terrible attrition.

To understand why and how this is happening, it is useful to look at some of the misunderstandings about language. An important distinction is the difference between an extinct language and a dead language. When many of the spoken languages of the Native American Indians were replaced as a result of colonialism by English, French, Spanish or Portuguese, they became extinct. A dead language may share many features with an extinct language, but a crucial distinction is that there may be situations where a dead language still serves a purpose. Typical examples would be the use of the language in special scientific, legal or religious contexts. Latin, by this definition, is dead but not extinct. Let us take this example further. It is true that Latin has no living native speakers, and no children learn it at their mother's breast. Yet it is still studied in schools and universities, and the literature is still available and widely read, though that is not sufficient to bring it to life. In linguistic terms, the Latin spoken by the soldiers, traders and settlers – Vulgar Latin, as opposed to the classical form spoken and written by the Roman upper classes – was subject to the normal process of change that languages commonly experience, and eventually developed into the family of Romance languages like French, Italian and Spanish. Old English similarly has no native speakers now, but did not become extinct: it simply morphed into Middle English, then Early Modern English and so on until it became the modern English we speak now.

Language has never been static. All living languages embody change, and always have done. It is in the nature of languages to change over time. This reflects the process by which each of us learns our own language. We can go beyond the obvious difference in language use between children and adults and assert that no two speakers of any language actually speak identically. People from different regions, even villages, sound different. Even within families and tightly knit speech communities, factors such as age, gender, education, intelligence, curiosity, openness to risk and new experiences result in slight differences in speech. Through encounters with others, we come across new words, different pronunciations, and subtly or explicitly these become integrated into our speech. These differences, tiny though they may individually be, taken together build a picture of language as being in a state of constant flux and development. As no one speaker ever speaks the entirety of the language in all its variants, with all its vocabulary, and no two speakers use the language identically, it follows that the language itself is a shifting force.

What we are witnessing today is a clear demonstration of what many find an uncomfortable truth. Languages compete for speakers. Dominant languages attract speakers to abandon minority languages for a variety of reasons, chiefly including prestige, education and employment. This happens over time, and often in several stages. For example, speakers may decide to replace elements of their mother tongue with something from the language they are attracted towards. And should their home language have some element that is absent from the new target language, speakers may drop it. There may even be a stage where speakers are functionally bilingual, but this will normally fade in favour of the dominant language in the process known as assimilation. This has not always been voluntary. In the past, conquering armies or administrations have subjugated a community and imposed the use of their language, perhaps on pain of death or other less severe consequences. Nowadays, it is largely cultural forces that are at work behind assimilation. In our global economy, languages with global reach offer more possibilities of every type. Local dialects and languages spoken in isolated communities are all at risk.

There are many cases of languages in terminal decline, with members of the younger generation no longer being able to have a conversation in the language of their grandparents because they have switched to a new, more global, less local language. In such cases, although the language is still spoken, it is moribund, and language death can be predicted with certainty as the transmission of the language from one generation to another has ended. This is normally a slow process that takes place over several generations, with each set of children learning less and less of the language of home. Finally, the language only exists in the domain of traditional use, where it might be recited in poetry or song, or used in religious or ritual contexts.

Should we be more worried? Precisely because language death is a natural phenomenon, many believe little can be done to prevent it, and we should let nature take its course. There are even voices that applaud the logic of a move towards a single global language, a unifying force that they claim would put an end to misunderstandings between nations and individuals.

What is lost when a language ceases to exist? Languages constitute immense stores of accumulated human knowledge derived from thousands of years of experience. In these times of instant messaging via email, texts and Twitter, it may come as a surprise to learn that most languages through history have not been written down at all, but have lived in the cultures, routines and memories of people who have developed the skills and strategies that have enabled them to create systems of survival appropriate to the environments and circumstances they inhabit. These languages are records of the plants and animals the people shared their environment with, the ways they were used or feared. They can be compared to catalogues of stories, weather patterns, social norms, local traditions, songs, sayings, ways of living, loving, fighting, and conducting trade and business. For linguists, languages are much more than collections of words. Above all, they are records of cultural heritage and ways of expressing a community's relationships with nature, between themselves and the wider world.

7 Read the text again and answer these questions.

Questions 1–5

Choose the correct letter, ***A***, ***B***, ***C*** *or* ***D***.

1 In the first paragraph, the writer expresses surprise that
A so many languages are in the process of disappearing.
B not many people seem concerned about the loss of languages.
C language change appears to be speeding up.
D there are still so many languages being spoken.

2 According to the writer, the main difference between dead and extinct languages is
A nobody speaks dead languages.
B extinct languages are not studied at school or university.
C there are situations when dead languages are used.
D extinct languages tried to resist the normal process of change.

3 The attraction of dominant languages is
A they are easier to learn than minority languages.
B people can practise elements of them at home.
C they appear to offer a better life to their speakers.
D they encourage people to be bilingual.

4 A language may be considered in terminal decline
A when different generations cannot understand one another.
B in cases where several generations each have fewer children.
C unless children are interested in traditions such as poetry and song.
D if grandchildren have not learned the language of their grandparents.

5 Language loss is serious because
A we lose the ability to read and understand the old languages.
B each language can teach us a unique history of life in one part of the world.
C some languages are not suited to modern forms of communication.
D it is not something we should think of as a natural process.

Pick from a list

In this question form, you have to pick correct answers from a list. You will be asked to pick a number of answers from a list of options – perhaps three answers from between six and eight options. The answers may not be in text order.

- Read the rubric carefully to make sure you know how many answers you are expected to give.
- It helps to underline the key words in each question that help you identify the sort of information required. The answers may be based on specific information, in which case you should underline the key words in the text.
- The answers may also be based on a understanding of the author's opinion, so you need to read the text carefully.
- Check that your answers match the number of answers stated in the rubric.

8 Underline the key words in the question and options below, then do the task.

Which ***THREE*** *of the following things are mentioned in the text?*

A How an app functions
B What application software may be used for
C The length of time that apps have existed
D The bright future of application software
E Who writes the apps
F The percentage of people using mobile apps
G The problems associated with use of mobile apps

Apps
Application software has been around for decades and allows the user to perform various tasks, such as document manipulation or modification of digital images. With the advent of more powerful mobile phones, a huge new field of mobile applications, or apps, has developed. Many apps are written by enthusiasts and are available for free. Others are developed by companies and given away for free in the hope that you will upgrade to an app which is not free, but with better features or with no advertising. For apps that are not free, the money is normally divided between the app developer (around 75%) and the distribution provider (around 25%). Games are one of the most popular apps, with over 90% of smartphone users playing a mobile game at least once a week.

Comments

A Incorrect: There is no mention of how an app functions. You are unlikely to get a very technical description in the IELTS test.
B Correct: Document manipulation, modification of digital images and games are mentioned.
C Correct: The first line states that *application software has been around for decades.*
D Incorrect: While apps certainly appear to have a bright future, there is no mention of it in the text. Be careful not to make judgements based on your own general knowledge rather than what is in the text.
E Correct: Both enthusiasts and companies are mentioned as writers of apps.
F Incorrect: While some percentage figures are given, they don't refer to the percentage of people using mobile apps.
G Incorrect: There is no mention of the problems associated with the use of mobile apps.

9 Now look back at the text on language on pages 38–39 and do this task.

Questions 6–8

Choose ***THREE*** *letters,* ***A–G****.*

The list below gives some reasons for language change.
Which ***THREE*** *reasons are mentioned by the writer of the text?*

A occupation or control by powerful foreign nations
B modern methods of communication
C the desire each person feels to be different
D an agreed need for a global language
E the influence of our contacts with others
F the natural consequence of the passage of time
G the increasing demand for bilingual speakers

Vocabulary builder 2

Prepositional phrases

A good way of improving your fluency in English is to make a collection of useful prepositional phrases. They are a regular feature of all types of speaking and writing and often form key 'chunks' of a text. Every time you read a text, make a list of useful new expressions with prepositions.

1 Complete these sentences with the correct prepositions. Check your answers by looking for the bold phrases in the text on pages 38–39 (they are not all in sequence), then find five more useful examples in the text.

1 There are a number of **ways** .... looking at this question.
2 We are .... **the process of** changing our computers.
3 We plan to introduce these changes .... **stages**.
4 There are considerable **differences** .... ability between adults and children learning new languages.
5 Planning what you want to say generally **results** .... a more effective message.
6 Children often learn new languages easily, **as opposed** .... adults, who tend to slave away with books and private lessons.
7 The company **developed** .... several years into a worldwide business.
8 We are **moving** .... a situation where all communication will take place virtually.

Organizing words

2 Add these organizing words and expressions to the correct categories in the table below. One expression may fit in more than one category.

1 on top of that 2 meanwhile 3 likewise 4 in short
5 as follows 6 claim 7 hence 8 whereas

describing procedures	*the next step, once you have done that, at this point*
time sequences	*initially, at first, subsequently, thereafter, finally*
giving examples	*such as, for instance, to give an example, to illustrate the point, by way of example, a case in point, as is witnessed by, proof of this*
discussing results	*consequently, as a result*
comparing	*alike, in the same manner, similarly, not only ... but also, in the same vein, of a similar nature, correspondingly, a further instance, a related case, more or less, not in the least, to a lesser degree*
contrasting	*actually, however, yet, in contrast, on the other hand, alternatively, differ from, although*
adding information	*additionally, in addition, what's more, besides, moreover, in the same vein*
reporting information	*according to, assert, maintain, argue a case, make a case, present an argument, believe*
concluding	*to sum up, in conclusion, thus, finally*
summarizing	*in a word, to sum up, all in all, taken as a whole*

3 Chose the most logical continuation (A–D) of each of these sentences.

1 Before man went into space, many animals were launched into orbit; for instance ...
  A they were testing to see if man could cope with the conditions.
  B a dog.
  C fruit flies, a dog and a chimpanzee.
  D using a rocket and a parachute.

2 Many people were concerned about the possible health risks of mobile-phone masts. Consequently ...
  A there was a series of masts built all over the country.
  B masts were disguised as trees.
  C the health risks were never investigated.
  D many people were not concerned about the problem any more.

3 Many people think of Morse code as being a slow method of communication, but actually it ...
  A is used by the US Navy.
  B is both speedy and effective when used by experts.
  C is widely used by many people around the world.
  D was invented by Thomas Edison.

4 Although ...
  A mobile phones are expensive and are frequently stolen by thieves.
  B fax machines are no longer used as email is cheaper and faster.
  C forms of social media such as Twitter are comparatively new, they have become an important means of communication.
  D people in Africa have an opportunity to use their mobile phones as a bank account.

5 Not only do many people pay high roaming charges for their mobile phones, they also ...
  A have problems understanding the rates offered by the various companies.
  B enjoy high-speed internet connection.
  C travel to many different countries.
  D have many applications which can help them find their destination.

Comments

1 *For instance* implies that there will be some examples, which is not the case in A or D. In B, only one example is given, so the correct answer is C.
2 The word *consequently* shows that the results will be described. A and C are not consequences, and D is illogical, so B is the correct answer.
3 The word *actually* implies that you are contrasting something and A, C and D are not. B is the correct answer, as it contrasts *slow* with *speedy*.
4 The word *although* implies a contrast. In D, only one thing is mentioned. In A, there are two things mentioned, but they are not being contrasted. In B, two things are mentioned and they are being contrasted, but the sentence structure doesn't work with *although*. Only C is the correct answer.
5 *Not only ... (but) also* tells us that further similar information is coming. The first part of the sentence is something bad (high roaming charges) and in B, C and D, the second parts are all positive, so the answer is A.

CLASSROOM WORKOUT

Them and us

- Work in groups. Each group chooses a different continent.
- In your groups, do some research using encyclopaedias, newspapers or magazines, and online sources to find:
  - which animals are in danger of disappearing on that continent, and why
  - what arguments there are for protecting these animals.
- Prepare a presentation to the other groups about what you have found.
- Have a class vote on the most effective means of protecting the animals.

CHECK YOURSELF

- Make a list of 10–15 different prefixes. For each prefix, try to find three different useful words.
- Write down five facts you know about different forms of communication as a result of reading the texts in this unit.

SUMMARY

In this unit, you:

- looked at communication collocations. How many did you write in your notebook?
- read about whale communication. Are you optimistic or pessimistic about the future of whales?
- studied word-building with prefixes. This is a great way to expand your vocabulary. What can you do to continue learning new words with prefixes?
- read about topic sentences and controlling ideas. How can this help you find an answer in the text?
- studied 'matching headings' questions. Why is it important to read the whole text before choosing an answer in this task type?
- looked at prepositional phrases. These are useful when you see language in chunks rather than as individual words and can help speed up your reading. How many were new for you?
- looked at organizing words. These will help you get a better idea of the flow of a text and aid prediction. If you have a good idea of what is coming next, then you have a better chance of understanding the whole text. How many expressions were new to you?

Over to you

1 Have a discussion with your friends about which forms of communication you think are most and least important.
2 Go online and find out about what forms of communication might be available soon.
3 Find a newspaper or magazine article or an online debate where people discuss advantages and disadvantages of social media and make a note of their arguments.

UNIT 4 Work and money

In this unit, you will:
- discuss the skills needed for different jobs
- study and practise **matching names**
- study and practise **matching sentence endings**.

Getting started

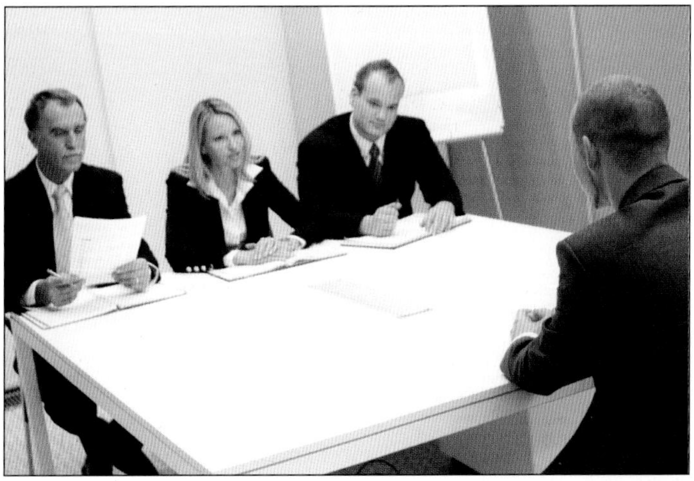

1 How do you think the people in the photo are feeling?

2 A job interview can be a difficult experience. Which of these ideas would you recommend to a friend before an interview?

- Do your homework and read up on the company history; make sure you check its marketing materials and mission statement before the interview so you can make some reference to them. Give some serious thought to what questions you can ask about the company and the job during the interview.
- Invest in some new clothes so you make a good impression at the interview. Do your best to look smart. If your clothes are coming apart at the seams, so will your hopes of getting the job.
- Have a look in a mirror before you make your way into the interview room. All your good work will come to nothing if they remember you for the piece of spinach stuck to your teeth.
- Prepare for the sort of questions most likely to come up: your strengths, what qualifies you for the job, reasons for leaving your current position. If asked about weaknesses you may have, come clean about a time when you tried to do too much – but don't tell them how you made a mess of your last relationship.
- Look the interviewer in the eyes and give him or her a strong, confident handshake. You're the kind of person who gets results – that's the message you want to give.
- Make a deliberate effort to find out the name of the interviewer and use it on several occasions during the interview.
- Make it clear that you are ambitious and are determined to work hard to get to the top and run your own business one day.
- If the interviewer makes a joke, laugh loudly to show that you've got a great sense of humour, and that you can get on well with people.
- Don't make the mistake of arriving with just minutes to spare. Give yourself plenty of time.
- Be modest about your skills. You don't want to come across as arrogant.
- Make a point of informing the interviewer of all your talents. You get things done and you've got a good business head.

3 Read the advice again and make a list of useful expressions with these verbs.

1 come 2 do 3 get 4 give 5 make

4 It's a good idea to keep a list of expressions with common verbs. What expressions do you know with these verbs?

1 go 2 find 3 take

Vocabulary builder 1

Jobs and professions

1 Put these jobs and professions into what you consider to be the correct categories in the table below. Each one may appear in more than one category, or they may not appear in any.

chemical engineer firefighter mental-health nurse shopkeeper portrait photographer professional football player ballet dancer politician carpenter social worker history teacher dentist computer programmer

require a lot of natural talent	require a lot of study/training	likely to be in great demand in the future	not given the recognition they deserve

2 Which three of the jobs in Exercise 1 would you most like to do? Which three jobs would you least like to do? Why?

3 Match each sentence beginning (1–12) to the correct ending (a–l).

1 I have to make important decisions ...
2 It doesn't take a lot of courage to visit me ...
3 I joined because I hoped and still hope ...
4 It came as a shock to my parents ...
5 I plan in detail because there's so much ...
6 My motivation is not to make a fortune ...
7 Helping people deal with problems is stressful ...
8 I work long hours, but I always find the time ...
9 It's physically demanding, and takes a lot of practice ...
10 I enjoy working with people ...
11 My time is taken up with research into new food products ...
12 Working on efficient software solutions involves expertise ...

a ... that can help feed the planet safely.
b ... but to work with my hands.
c ... as it really is a painless experience these days.
d ... in different subjects such as algorithms and formal logic.
e ... and creating something with lasting memories for them.
f ... that I was earning so much so young.
g ... yet incredibly rewarding at the same time.
h ... to make a big difference to people's lives.
i ... to get to the top of the profession.
j ... to talk to customers, as it's part of the service.
k ... that can go wrong in a lesson.
l ... that can be matters of life and death.

4 Which job(s) from Exercise 1 do you associate with each statement in Exercise 3?

Spotlight on exam skills 1

Identifying what is required

When you are looking for the answer to a question, there is a lot of text to consider and you do not have time to re-read the whole text for each question. It is vital that you identify exactly what you are looking for – this will make the task of finding the right answer a lot easier. Check the questions and pay attention to whether you need to find a fact, a name, a number, an opinion or something else, and whether the answer is a singular or a plural, a present or a past, etc.

1 Underline the key words in these questions which indicate what sort of answer to look for. Then suggest what the answer could be – this will help your prediction skills.

1 In addition to banks, where do people in Switzerland invest their money?
2 What happens to British bank accounts that are dormant for more than 15 years?
3 What, according to Dr King, was the most important factor which led to the banking crisis?
4 According to the text, who are the main instigators of banking changes in Uganda?
5 Which are the two most important decisions facing a couple planning to take out a mortgage?
6 How many people in Nigeria use their mobile phone to access their bank account?
7 What difficulties did the team have to overcome before they could start their business?
8 How were small businesses in Denmark affected by the introduction of a new business tax?

2 Look in your dictionary and find five expressions with *work* that you think are useful.

Looking at words in context

In the text on page 48 about employment in Australia, there are a number of words and expressions which may not be familiar to you.
Here are tips to help you guess the meaning of unfamiliar words or expressions.

1 Read the paragraph that the word or expression appears in so you know the topic and general focus of the text.
2 Focus closely on the sentence with the new word or expression. Read the words around the new item(s) and check the grammar. What part of speech is the new word or expression?
3 If it's a verb, does it seem to be a verb of motion, possession, emotion, speech, change, etc.?
4 If it's an adjective, does it seem to relate to quality, dimension, material, character, origin, etc.?
5 If it's a noun, does it seem to be concrete or abstract, a type of person, category of object, etc.?
6 Try to guess whether it has a generally positive or negative meaning.
7 Look at the grammar: is the verb present or past? Is it active or passive?
8 Look at how the word is formed. Words with prefixes such as *de-*, *il-*, *im-*, *un-* are likely to have an idea of negativity or absence. Words with suffixes such as *-ation*, *-ivity*, *-sis* are likely to relate to abstracts, qualities, processes, etc. If the word is part of a longer expression, does it seem to be literal or idiomatic?
9 Sometimes you can guess the meaning because the word will relate to another word or idea in the text, and may be a synonym, an opposite or an example.
10 Pay attention to sound, too. Often the sound of a word can give an impression of something heavy, unpleasant, loud, etc. – or the opposite.

Employees working longer to keep jobs

Australians are being asked to work longer hours as bosses delay hiring new staff in the biggest jobs slowdown in two decades, new data from the Australian Bureau of Statistics reveals.

Almost 30,000 workers were **turfed out** of their jobs in the lead-up to Christmas, with many who kept their jobs asked to shoulder an ever-increasing **burden**, the *Herald Sun* reports, as employers have been asking staff to work longer hours rather than taking on new workers

'While there is less work available, we are also working harder, with the number of hours worked rising by 0.3 per cent in December,' Commsec chief economist Craig James said. Mr James **tipped** unemployment to rise to as high as 5.7 per cent this year.

'After holding out for the past six months, Aussie businesses have finally decided to **bite the bullet**. They have to, and that's why they have started **culling** staff – albeit modestly.'

The data came as acting Treasurer Bill Shorten warned that more jobs could be lost if conditions in Europe worsen. 'There is a tough year ahead of us in Australia, with big challenges in the global economy, which will inevitably impact on our economy,' he said.

The fall in employment in December surprised many economists who were forecasting an increase of 10,000 jobs. Part-time workers were hit hard in the lead-up to Christmas, with 53,700 stripped of employment. The figures showed full-time employment was up 24,500 last month. The unemployment figure actually remained stable on 5.2 per cent nationally, as fewer people looked for work. Mr James said the **dour** figures would force the Reserve Bank's hand for a February rate cut from the current 4.25 per cent.

adapted from www.news.com.au

3 Read the passage and then choose the correct options for each of the words in bold.

1 **Turfed out** is **a)** *a noun / a verb* and seems **b)** *positive / negative.*

It means:

A given extra money.

B given less money.

C dismissed.

D head-hunted.

2 **Burden** is **a)** *a noun / an adjective* and seems **b)** *positive / negative.*

It means:

A money.

B load.

C time.

D work.

3 **Tipped** is a verb of *speaking / emotion.*

It means:

A gave advice.

B predicted.

C worried.

D wrote on a keyboard.

4 **Bite the bullet** is **a)** *literal / idiomatic* and seems **b)** *positive / negative.*
It means:
A choose to do something unpleasant.
B take a risk.
C feel positive about the future.
D do something illegal.

5 **Culling** is a verb of **a)** *action / thinking* and seems **b)** *positive / negative.*
It means:
A getting rid of.
B employing.
C behaving badly towards.
D supporting.

6 **Dour** is an adjective of **a)** *quality / size* and seems **b)** *positive / negative.*
It means
A impressive.
B long term.
C unexpected.
D depressing.

4 Match each source of information (1–3) with the correct statement below (A–E). There are two statements which do not match any of the sources.

1 Craig James
2 *Herald Sun*
3 Bill Shorten

A Economic changes in other countries will influence the situation in Australia.
B There are fewer job vacancies being advertised at present.
C Workers are being put under pressure to work more.
D Further increases in the number of people without work are likely.
E The problem of unemployment affects some groups of workers particularly harshly.

Dealing with unknown words

5 Try the following to improve your ability to deal with unknown words.

- Each day this week, find an article online or from a suitable newspaper or magazine that contains 10–15 words or expressions that you don't know.
- Spend ten minutes guessing what the words mean without using a dictionary. Then see how accurate your guesses were.
- Keep a score of how many words you guess more or less correctly each day.

If your score improves from day 1 to day 7, well done. We recommend that you continue to practise like this once a week. If your score has not improved much, then continue with daily practice for two more weeks.

Vocabulary builder 2

Paraphrase practice

Effective readers have large vocabularies. One of the keys to success in IELTS is to develop a large vocabulary of synonyms.

1 Match the words on the left (1–19) to those on the right (a–s) that have the same or similar meanings.

1 lucrative	a lack
2 employer	b wrong
3 reason	c produce
4 mistaken	d belief
5 shortage	e outcome
6 manufacture	f characteristic
7 normally	g profitable
8 artificial	h undertake
9 result	i attribute
10 basis	j factory owner
11 partly	k in part
12 opinion	l various
13 perform	m motive
14 often	n foundation
15 several	o start
16 feature	p man-made
17 essential	q regularly
18 create	r vital
19 ascribe	s generally

2 This paragraph contains many words or expressions that have similar meanings to those in Exercise 1. How many can you find?

Any economist will agree that entrepreneurs are crucial to the development of every branch of industry. Frequently, the most successful are those serial entrepreneurs who have set up multiple businesses in the course of their careers. Research traditionally explains the success of these individuals who find themselves bosses of a string of prosperous businesses in terms of traits such as risk-taking and competitiveness. However, genetic analysis carried out in America suggests that this view may be erroneous, or at best only true to a certain extent. According to some social scientists, serial entrepreneurs are actually distinguished more by their sociability. Their findings are the first attempt to demonstrate that business success could have genetic roots. This represents a new approach to how to understand this category of entrepreneurs and the driving force behind their innovations.

3 In each of these sentences, decide if the word in brackets has the same meaning as the word in bold.

1 The new visa restrictions could have **far-reaching** consequences for companies involved in international travel. (*serious*)
2 News of local terrorist activity unsurprisingly had a dramatic **impact** on hotel bookings. (*influence*)
3 The government is **reluctant** to increase taxes again. (*planning*)
4 There have been **further** complications. (*additional*)
5 After a successful career in banking, he **eventually** went on to become a politician. (*fortunately*)
6 Industry leaders agree that the decline in educational standards is a growing **problem**. (*issue*)
7 Price rises would be likely to **reduce** demand for our products. (*boost*)
8 In most countries, there is a **stigma** attached to being declared bankrupt. (*reward*)
9 The situation has **recently** started to show signs of improvement. (*lately*)
10 A period of work experience can **enhance** your CV in the eyes of future employers. (*improve*)

Choosing words from a list

Some of the exercises in the IELTS test require you to complete sentences or notes using words from a list. There are generally more words in the list than there are gaps, so you have to read carefully. Use these tips to help you.

1 Read the text and check what type(s) of word are required to fill each gap – nouns, verbs, adjectives, numbers, etc.
2 See how many of each type of word there are in the box, and see which fits best in the gap.
3 Check if you can use a word or phrase more than once.
4 Make sure you spell the words correctly when writing the answers.

4 Complete the text below using words and phrases from the box. There are more choices than gaps, so you will not need to use all of them.

as an advantage bankruptcies computer creation deposit account
doing well entrepreneurs failures for a change for the best happily
international job losses large managers managing proliferation
rise redundancy cheque struggling suffering

No matter how difficult the business climate is, there is always some good that can come from tough trading conditions. Although 1 .... are obviously a very unwelcome sign that a business is not 2 .... , surprisingly, they can, in the long term, sometime work out 3 .... If 4 .... companies are forced to lose people, the result can be a 5 .... of small companies starting up, as talented 6 .... turn an idea into a business, often funded by a 7 ....

5 Think of three different ways of summarizing the key ideas of the text in Exercise 4, focusing on:

1 entrepreneurs
2 redundancy cheques
3 tough trading conditions.

Spotlight on exam skills 2

Matching names

1 You have to relate information to a number of people, places, categories or theories, etc.
2 Look at the list of names, then scan the text to find them. Underline them in the text.
3 Remember that names may appear in several places in the text.
4 Check the instructions to see if names can be matched with just one or more than one option.
5 There may be distractors that do not match any name.

1 Read this text and choose the most suitable heading for each paragraph (A–D).

Bye, bye banknote

The End of Money by David Wolman, reviewed by Jacob Aron

A *Money in all its forms / No money in my pocket / Is money evil?*
Cash, dough or moolah – whatever you call it, you can't live without it. Or can you? Increasingly money is an abstraction residing on a computer drive. How long will it be until hard currency disappears altogether? In *The End of Money*, journalist David Wolman sets out to discover what a cashless world might look like and how we will arrive there. On the way, he gets distracted by those on the fringes of society. The book opens with Glenn Guest, a US pastor who believes credit cards and online banking are tools of Satan, designed to bring about the end of the world. An entertaining notion, but not relevant to anyone just fed up with carrying a chunk of change.

B *Cash and crime / Loose change / Currencies and copies*
Later, Wolman visits Bernard von NotHaus, creator of the Liberty Dollar currency. Until 2009, it was available electronically, in note form and as coins – though von NotHaus denied they were coins, which he says only governments can mint. Such semantic wrangling failed to prevent him being found guilty of counterfeiting. It's not surprising, as the Liberty Dollar closely mimics many features of the US dollar, using 'Trust in God' instead of 'In God we Trust' for example. It seems odd to focus on such a strange character when, as Wolman points out, alternative currencies such as the Brixton Pound in London succeed without falling foul of the law.

C *The cost of cash / Social consequences / Crime pays*
The book is better when focusing on the real implications of moving away from cash: a particularly good chapter details the mobile-banking revolution in the developing world, which is allowing countries such as Kenya to leapfrog the need for expensive ATM and banking infrastructure. Interesting, too, are the arguments for abolishing cash, such as the fact that making hard currency is a costly business, as much as 1 per cent of annual Gross Domestic Product for some countries. Cash is used to prop up crime: high-value bills provide an anonymous way to conduct illicit transactions. UK exchange offices no longer take €500 notes after an inquiry found that nine in every ten of them were used by criminals.

D *Alternative banking systems / Technological money / The future is here*
So what might replace cash? Wolman touches on energy as a unit of currency, and whizzes through virtual currencies like World of Warcraft gold, Facebook credits and Bitcoin, suggesting conversion software could let people pay using whatever they have to hand. Ultimately, though, one gets the feeling that the cashless society is already with us, at least for those that want it. Early in the book, Wolman mentions his attempt to avoid cash for an entire year, but other than a few awkward moments when splitting restaurant bills or passing lemonade stands, he rarely refers to it again – perhaps because parting with your cash is easier than you might expect.

adapted from *New Scientist*

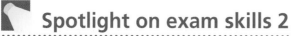

2 Decide which category (A–E) each of the statements below (1–8) falls into. You may use any letter more than once.

A a fact or an opinion expressed by David Wolman
B a fact or an opinion expressed by Jacob Aron
C a fact or an opinion expressed by Glenn Guest
D a fact or an opinion expressed Bernard von NotHaus
E a fact or an opinion not expressed in the text

1 Not having cash could reduce costs of government.
2 No individual has the right to make coins.
3 No society can manage without money.
4 Not all alternatives to official currencies are illegal.
5 Nobody should use credit cards.
6 No computers are designed to manage our money.
7 Nobody actually needs to use cash now.
8 Nothing is more dangerous than carrying cash with you.

3 Complete these sentences using no more than TWO WORDS AND/OR A NUMBER from the text for each answer.

1 One of the questions the book asks is how near is the time when we will live in a society that is ....
2 Von NotHaus was unsuccessful in defending himself against the charge of ....
3 In developing countries, people are using technology creatively to avoid the difficulties and expense involved in establishing a ....
4 As research in the UK indicates their attraction to those involved in crime, some high-value notes cannot be accepted in ....

Word building

4 a Without using your dictionary, look at the text and explain what these expressions mean.

Paragraph A
1 hard currency
2 sets out
3 on the way
4 the fringes of society

Paragraph B
5 mint (a coin)
6 semantic wrangling
7 falling foul of

Paragraph C
8 to leapfrog the need for
9 a costly business
10 to prop up (crime)

Paragraph D
11 touches on
12 whizzes through
13 have to hand

b Now check in your dictionary to see if you were right.

5 Discuss with your colleagues the advantages and disadvantages of:

1 cash
2 cheques
3 credit cards
4 money alternatives such as bartering.

Matching sentences

> This task type tests your understanding of the main ideas in a text.

6 You are going to read a text about an important development in the theory of management. Before you read, discuss what you know about the following.

1 Henry Ford
2 mass production
3 how to motivate workers
4 the need for flexibility at work
5 the relationship between managers and workers

7 Read the text to check what it says about the topics in Exercise 6.

Scientific Management in the workplace

The car and computer manufacturing plants, the work environments we go to every day, the hospitals we are treated in, and even some of the restaurants we might eat in all function more efficiently due to the application of methods that come from Scientific Management. In fact, these methods of working seem so commonplace and so logical to a citizen of the modern world that it is almost impossible to accept that they were revolutionary only 100 years ago.

Scientific Management was developed in the first quarter of the 20th century; its father is commonly accepted to be F.W. Taylor. Taylor recognized labor productivity was largely inefficient due to a workforce that functioned by "rules of thumb." Taylor carried out studies to ensure that factual scientific knowledge would replace these traditional "rules of thumb." The backbone of this activity was his "time-and-motion study." This involved analyzing all the operations and the motions performed in a factory, and timing them with a stopwatch. By knowing how long it took to perform each of the elements of each job, he believed it would be possible to determine a fair day's work.

Work, he contended, was more efficient when broken down into its constituent parts, and the management, planning, and decision-making functions had been developed elsewhere. As this implies, Taylor viewed the majority of workers as ill-educated and unfit to make important decisions about their work.

Taylor's system ensured the most efficient way would be used by all workers, therefore making the work process standard. Invariably, managers found that maximal efficiency was achieved by a subdivision of labor. This subdivision entailed breaking the workers' tasks into smaller and smaller parts. In short, he specified not only what was to be done, but also how it was to be done and the exact time allowed for doing it.

One theory based on the Scientific Management model is Fordism. This theory refers to the application of Henry Ford's faith in mass production—in his case, of cars—and combined the idea of the moving assembly line with Taylor's systems of division of labor and piece-rate payment. With Fordism, jobs are automated or broken down into unskilled or semi-skilled tasks. The pace of the continuous-flow assembly line dictated work. But Ford's theory retained the faults of Taylor's. Autocratic management ensured a high division of labor in order to effectively run mass production; this led to little workplace democracy, and alienation. Equally, with emphasis on the continuous flow of the assembly line, machinery was given more importance than workers.

The benefits of Scientific Management lie within its ability provide a company with the focus to organize its structure in order to meet the objectives of both the employer and employee. Taylor found that the firms that introduced Scientific Management became the world's most carefully organized corporations.

Scientific Management, however, has been criticized for "de-skilling" labor. As jobs are broken down into their constituent elements, humans become little more than "machines" in the chain. Their cognitive input is not required: it is best if they do not have to think about their tasks. Yet the average intelligence of employees has risen sharply; people have been made aware of their value as human beings. They are no longer content to receive only financial reward for their tasks. It has been recognized that productivity and success are not just obtained by controlling all factors in the workplace, but by contributing to the social well-being and development of the individual employee.

Higher levels of access to technology and information, as well as increased competition, present another difficulty to theory of Scientific Management in the 21st century. Modern organizations process huge amounts of input, and employees no longer work in isolated units cut off from the organization at large. Managers recognize they are unable to control all aspects of employees' functions, as the number layers of information factored into everyday decisions is so high that it is imperative employees use their own initiative. High competition between organizations also means that companies must react fast to maintain market positions. All this forces modern companies to maintain high levels of flexibility.

In the era during which Scientific Management was developed, each worker had a specific task that he or she had to perform, with little or no real explanation of why, or what part it played in the organization as a whole. In this day and age, it is virtually impossible to find an employee in the developed world who is not aware of what his or her organization stands for, what their business strategy is, how well the company is performing, and what their job means to the company as a whole. Organizations actively encourage employees to know about their company and to work across departments, ensuring that communication at all levels is mixed and informal.

Another weakness in Scientific Management theory is that it can lead to workers becoming too highly specialized, therefore hindering their adaptability to new situations. Nowadays, employers not only want workers to be efficient, they must also exhibit flexibility.

In conclusion, it can be seen that Scientific Management is still very much part of organizations today. Its strengths in creating a divide between management functions and work functions have been employed widely at all levels and in all industries. In addition, its strengths in making organizations efficient through replacement of "rules of thumb" with scientific fact ensured its widespread application.

adapted from www.articlecity.com

8 Complete this task.

Questions 1–6

*Complete each sentence with the correct ending **A–H**.*

According to the article:

1 Productivity
2 Time-and-motion analysis
3 Decision-making
4 Subdivision of labour
5 Fordism
6 A worker

A meant a job was reduced to a number of basic elements.
B was considered undesirable in the role of the workers.
C became specialized in certain unchanging work routines.
D measured the exact time it took to do each part of a job.
E carefully calculated what was required for the success of a business.
F was an application of a theory to mass production.
G took a critical view of the style of management.
H suffered as a result of established inefficient practices.

Questions 7–14

*Complete this summary using the list of words **A–N** below.*

Scientific Management theories are responsible for many of the procedures in evidence in today's companies. The key to this was the **7** .... analysis of what each job involved in order to replace **8** .... with scientific knowledge. True efficiency could only be reached when the different processes in the workplace were made **9** .... Ford applied these principles to car production, where workers did specific jobs on the **10** .... However, the theory was criticized for viewing people as **11** .... , as they were expected to be able to perform their tasks without **12** .... Their motivation, according to the theory, was supposed to be simply **13** .... Nowadays, companies recognize that the best results also depend on other factors, such as promoting the **14** .... of the workers and their professional and personal development.

A labour productivity
B time-and-motion
C moving assembly line
D stopwatch
E thinking
F rules of thumb
G backbone
H de-skilling
I division of labour
J financial reward
K standard
L machines
M average intelligence
N social well-being

CLASSROOM WORKOUT

Paraphrase practice

- Work in pairs or small groups. How many different ways can you find in five minutes to paraphrase these sentences?
  1 Money is the cause of many serious problems in society.
  2 Having a good job is good for you and for society.
  3 A friend in need is a friend indeed.
  4 Society should provide work for its citizens.
- Now each pair/group writes a sentence on one of the topics of this unit on a piece of paper. Pass the piece of paper around the class. Each pair has to try to write a different paraphrase of the original sentence. When the piece of paper is back with the original writers, they must judge whether all the paraphrases are accurate enough to be acceptable.

CHECK YOURSELF

- Make a list of 10–15 collocations or expressions using the verbs *do*, *make* and *get* that you could use in a discussion on the topic of work.
- Re-read the texts in this unit and make a list of opinions about success at work.

SUMMARY

In this unit, you:

- looked at expressions with key verbs. How many did you write in your notebook?
- read about unemployment in Australia. Is the situation in your country the same or different?
- studied techniques for guessing the meaning of new words from the context. Read a newspaper article, count how many new words there are, and see how many you can guess. Then check in a dictionary.
- practised synonyms. How can this help you in the exam?
- studied 'matching names' questions. Why is it important to read the whole text before choosing an answer in this task type?
- studied 'sentence completion by matching' tasks. What does this task test?
- read about a cashless society. How attached are people in your country to the currency you have?

Over to you

1 Read an article in a newspaper or business magazine. Try to find at least 20 words for which you know synonyms.
2 Find and analyze the websites of leading national and multinational companies to see what they say about their working practices, results, job skills and vacancies.
3 Find and read a newspaper article about an aspect of world economics. What does it say about job creation or job losses?

UNIT 5 Society and social issues

In this unit, you will:
- discuss social issues
- study and practise **note completion**
- study and practise **summary completion**.

Getting started

1

2

3

4

5

6

7

8

9

1 Which photos do you associate most with these expressions?

a save for the future **b** law and order **c** democratic elections
d get a good education **e** earn a living **f** respect for one's elders
g your nearest and dearest **h** community spirit **i** keep body and soul together
j a sense of tradition **k** free-time activity **l** keeping up to date

2 Discuss these questions about the things represented in the photos.

1 What positive contribution does each make to society?
2 What can go wrong in society if they do not function properly?
3 How important is it for a society to know about its past?

3 Circle the odd one out in each list.

1 law-abiding citizen / career criminal / juvenile delinquent
2 get into debt / go bankrupt / live within your means
3 be out of work / have a good career / work your way to the top of the profession
4 a sense of belonging / membership of a group / nobody to turn to
5 pass your exams / drop out / do well at school
6 freedom of the press / press censorship / impose a news blackout

Vocabulary builder

Social issues

1 How many paired expressions about social issues can you make using these words?

Example: social issues

labour
sexual
rights
violence
immigrants
orientation
groups
illegal
hate
rates
pregnancy
domestic
underage
minorities
teenage
drug
social
crime
discrimination
minority
issues
unrest
ethnic
society
civilized
abuse
social
child
crimes
animal

2 Discuss these questions.

1 In your opinion, what are the most serious social issues affecting people where you live?

2 Which problems could be solved by the following?
- better education
- improved job opportunities
- greater respect for individuals
- more extensive healthcare

Word building

3 Rank these expressions according to how useful you think they are.

antisocial behaviour
high society
in today's society
know him socially
social climber
social engineering
social life
social skills
social work
socialite
unsocial hours

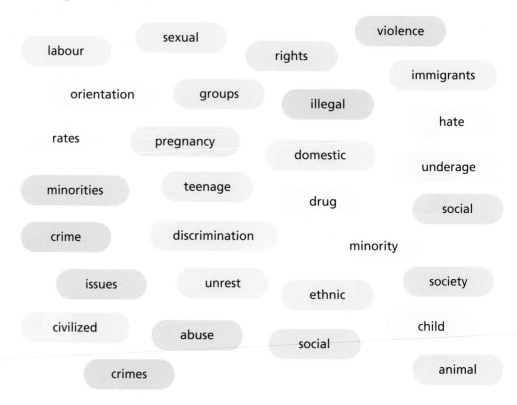

Spotlight on exam skills 1

Summary completion

1 Complete these extracts with expressions from Exercise 1 on page 58.

A

One of the **1** ...social issues... I feel most strongly about is **2** .... I don't think most young girls are ready to accept the responsibilities that go with motherhood. What's more, it almost guarantees that they will be unable to finish their education, and in all likelihood, that will have severe consequences for the sort of work they will be able to find, if any.

B

Police figures confirm that **3** .... have increased enormously over the past decade, with burglary and car theft rising dramatically in all areas of the country. While it is impossible to attribute this to one single cause, it is often pointed out that **4** .... is a frequent motive for crime, as addicts struggle to get money to feed their addiction, which is why it should be a top priority to address the issue of drugs.

C

A mark of any **5** .... is how it tolerates people from different backgrounds and people who have different lifestyles or viewpoints. We have made tremendous progress in dealing with intolerance of all sorts. The end of **6** .... in the workplace means that women are no longer paid less than men for the same job. Similarly, you can't discriminate against gay people on the grounds of their **7** .... These are positive steps.

D

I am fundamentally against exploitation in all its forms. It is therefore right that clothing companies should ensure that no children are involved in the manufacture of the clothes they sell because **8** .... robs the youngest and most vulnerable members of society of their childhood.

There are also other issues closer to home that rarely get the attention they deserve. The phenomenon of **9** .... is still huge, mostly husbands against wives, but there are cases where the wives are the guilty parties.

E

In a multicultural society, different communities have to learn to get along with one another. Most people would say that **10** .... bring colour and new perspectives that are to be welcomed. They tend to work hard, often doing the jobs we consider beneath us. But in times of unemployment, it is common for people to blame 'outsiders' and in particular **11** .... for taking 'our' jobs, and extremists call for them to be repatriated.

F

I don't think it's right that in the name of science we torture millions of innocent creatures just so we can have better cosmetics, shampoos or even medicines. The systematic mistreatment of dogs, cats, mice, rats, rabbits and others in this way is abuse, pure and simple, and we should be ashamed of it. Because I believe in **12** .... , I won't wear fur, either.

G

How tolerant are we really? We preach tolerance, the acceptance of those who differ from us, but the reality is that **13** .... occur every day in all our cities. People are insulted, attacked or worse for being black, or gay, or followers of a different religion. Ask any members of **14** .... and they will tell you they know someone who has experienced this personally, and that it makes them feel like second-class citizens.

H

Civil disturbance, the breakdown of law and order, is a symptom of deep problems in society and is often sparked by a single incident that comes after a lengthy period of **15** .... It can generally be understood as a form of protest. In many cases, peaceful demonstrations have become violent as a small group which may or may not be organized causes chaos by their actions, whether planned or unplanned.

Every sentence in a text serves a purpose. Each sentence in some way relates back to the previous one, for example by adding more information, giving a contrasting opinion or supporting an opinion with an example. Understanding how sentences relate to one another is a key reading skill. It is also very useful when completing notes or summaries.

2 Read the extracts in Exercise 1 again to find expressions that are examples of:

1 causes
2 consequences
3 facts
4 opinions
5 illustrations and examples
6 generalizations
7 definitions
8 predictions

These are common patterns in texts:

start with:		**move on to:**
general point		specific details
statement		qualification of the statement
opinion	→	support for the opinion
question		answer
problem		solution

3 Which of the above patterns can you find in the extracts in Exercise 1?

4 Complete these paragraphs so they are true for you.

In my country, one of the biggest social challenges we face at the moment is **1** .... (*issue*), which is **2** .... (*definition*). People say the solution could lie in **3** .... (*doing what?*). This would involve **4** .... (*which measures?*).

Societies are based on both trust and tradition. An example of this is **5** .... (*example of trust*). In my country, opinions are divided about traditions. Some people think it is important to keep traditions such as **6** .... (*example of tradition*). On the other hand, others do not worry so much when traditions are lost. To give an example, it is no longer common for young people in particular to **7** .... (*example of a tradition young people don't follow now*). What this shows is that **8** .... (*your interpretation of what is happening to traditions*). In my opinion, in the near future, it is likely that **9** .... (*prediction about future development*).

It is impossible for groups, individuals or societies to resist change. One problem these days is that change is happening more quickly than before as a result of **10** .... (*cause(s) of change*). Of course, for some people, this is unwelcome and may even represent a threat to values and a way of life they hold dear. These people are likely to try to protect the life they are familiar with by **11** .... (*actions they may take to do this*). Others, for example **12** .... (*groups who are in favour of change*), are more open to change.

5 Which social issues have appeared most recently in your national news? Summarize the stories, paying attention to who, where, what, why, when and how.

Exam practice

6 You should spend 20 minutes on this task.

I can put my cash card into an ATM anywhere in the world and take out a fistful of local currency, while the corresponding amount is debited from my bank account at home. I don't even think twice: regardless of the country, I trust that the system will work.

The whole world runs on trust. We trust that people on the street won't rob us, that the bank we deposited money in last month returns it this month, that the justice system punishes the guilty and exonerates the innocent. We trust the food we buy won't poison us, and the people we let in to fix our boiler won't murder us.

Society is an interdependent system that requires widespread co-operation to function. People need to act in ways that are expected of them, to be consistent and compliant. And not just individuals, but organizations and systems. But in any co-operative system, there is an alternative, parasitic strategy available – cheating. A parasite obtains the benefits of widespread co-operation while at the same time taking advantage of it. There are – and always will be – robbers, crooked banks and judges who take bribes. So how do we ensure that the parasites are kept to a small enough minority to not ruin everything for everyone?

The paradox is that it is in our collective interest to be trustworthy and to co-operate, while it is in our individual self-interest to be parasitic and defect, or cheat. If too many defect, society stops functioning, the crime rate soars, international banking collapses and judicial rulings become available for sale to the highest bidder. No one would trust anyone because there wouldn't be enough trust to go around.

If we can increase the benefits of co-operation or the costs of defection, we can induce people to act in the group interest because it is also in their self-interest. These mechanisms have been called societal pressures. A bank's reputation in the community is a societal pressure. So is the lock on the ATM that keeps criminals out.

In reality, there is a complex interplay of societal pressures. The most basic are moral systems regulating our own behaviour. Most of us try not to treat others unfairly because it makes us feel bad and we know they will treat us badly in return. Most don't steal because we feel guilty – and there are consequences when we are caught. We recognize it is in our long-term self-interest not to act in our immediate self-interest.

Morals and reputation worked well enough for primitive lifestyles, but these began to fail as society grew too large. Trust is personal and intimate among people who know each other, and morals and reputation are easily limited to an in-group. Institutional systems – laws – formalized reputational systems, and security technologies allowed societal pressures to scale up as we expanded into ever-larger groups.

This trust isn't absolute, of course. Not every societal pressure affects everyone equally. Some care more about their reputations, others are naturally law-abiding and still others are better at picking locks. But the goal isn't total compliance, just to limit the scope for defection. Criminals still target ATMs, and the occasional rogue bank employee steals money from accounts. But for the most part, societal pressures keep defector damage small enough to keep the system intact.

But sometimes the scope is too great, and underlying systems come crashing down. Overfishing has destroyed breeding stocks in many places. Crime and corruption have devastated some countries. The international banking system almost collapsed in 2008. But in general, societal pressures work as a delicate balance between co-operation and defection. The balance isn't static – technological changes disrupt it all the time. The changes can be related to defecting, so ATM-based 'card-skimmers' make it easier for criminals to steal my codes and empty my bank account. Or they may be related to security, with computerized auditing technology making it more difficult for fraudulent transactions to go through the system unnoticed.

Life becomes dangerous and insecure when new technologies, innovations and ideas increase the scope of defection. Defectors innovate. New attacks become possible. Existing attacks become easier, cheaper, more reliable or more devastating. More people may defect, simply because it's easier to. In response, society must also innovate, to reduce the scope of defection and restore the balance. This dynamic is as old as civilization.

Global banking, terrorists with nuclear weapons, genetic engineering, bio-weapons, pandemics: we now have such dangerous systems that a few defectors can wreak havoc so great that reactive rebalancing might not be enough. Worse still, by the time that society realizes the gravity of the situation, irreversible damage may already have been done.

To add to the complexity, not all defectors are bad. Neither co-operation nor defection relate to any absolute standard of morality. It is defectors who are in the vanguard for change, such as those who helped escaped slaves in the US before the civil war. It is defectors who agitate to overthrow the repressive regimes they live under.

How to achieve the balance is at the core of many of our debates about introducing laws to police the Internet. Anonymity is essential to freedom and liberty and saves the lives of dissidents everywhere. Yet it also protects criminals. Copyright both protects and stifles innovation. The big challenge will be to understand how to simultaneously provide both more societal pressure to deal with the threats of technology, and less pressure to ensure an open, free and evolving society.

adapted from *New Scientist*

Question 1

The list gives some of the problems faced by a society based on trust.
*Which two problems are mentioned by the writer? Choose **TWO** letters **A–E**.*

A The difficulties of relying on international co-operation.
B The rewards for experienced criminals will always prove a temptation.
C The developments of technology can make criminal activity easier.
D The measures that could be used to control crime could also limit our freedoms.
E The cost of trying to prevent all forms of cheating is too high.

Questions 2–5

*Choose the correct letter **A**, **B**, **C** or **D**.*

2 We tend to act in a trusting and co-operative way because
A the collective interest is greater than our individual interest.
B group and individual interest are generally equal.
C the consequences of cheating are too great.
D it is in our nature to act in a moral manner.

3 The writer says that trust is limited because
A it does not include our opinions of the law.
B we only trust those we are familiar with.
C it is linked to our personal reputation.
D it is likely that cheats do not trust anyone.

4 The examples of overfishing and the problem of the banking system show that
A problems affect both society and the natural world.
B the system of trust is not reliable.
C the balance between co-operation and cheating is always at risk.
D people who cheat the system will sometimes have an advantage.

5 According to the writer, defectors from the system
A find it increasingly easy to cheat.
B can hope to achieve positive solutions to problems.
C are generally intelligent and innovative.
D try to do as much damage as possible.

Question 6

Which of the following is the most suitable title for the text?

A The impossibility of co-operation in a world of cheats
B The increased threats to a functioning society
C How to keep criminals in check for the benefit of society
D The importance of technology in balancing risk and reward in society
E The complexities of a society based on trust

Questions 7–10

Complete the summary of the third paragraph below.
*Choose no more than **THREE** words from the passage for each gap.*

Society is a network of related elements that depend on one another. What holds society together and enables it to work effectively is the **7** .... of its members. For this to happen, it is important that people behave as **8** .... , which applies equally to **9** .... However, some may aim to abuse this system for their own benefit by **10** .... These are the parasites who enjoy the fruits of co-operation while exploiting it selfishly for their purposes.

Comments

Q1

Answer: C, D

C *(... ATM-based 'card skimmers' and 'new technologies' ... increase the scope of defection.)*

D *(Anonymity is essential to freedom and liberty ... Yet it also protects criminals.)*

A is not mentioned at all. B may be understood, but is not mentioned; E is not specifically mentioned, though logical, as the text says the goal is not to make everyone comply, but to limit the scope for cheating.

Q2

A Correct. This is the paradox mentioned in the fourth paragraph.

B Incorrect. It is contradicted in the text

C Incorrect. It is mentioned as one example regarding stealing, not as a general fact, and human nature is not mentioned.

D Incorrect. We have learnt to balance collective and personal interest as society has grown – it is not nature.

Q3

A Incorrect. Although the law is mentioned several times, our opinion is not the focus.

B Correct.

C Incorrect: Reputation is mentioned as a means of regulating small groups.

D Incorrect: The trust of cheats is not mentioned.

Q4

A Incorrect: These are used as examples of the bigger problem of maintaining a balance between co-operation and cheating.

B Incorrect: The system is not discussed in terms of reliability.

C Correct. The balance isn't static.

D Incorrect: Although it is true technology gives cheats an advantage, the purpose of the example is to show the scale of the problem, not the means by which it was achieved.

Q5

A Incorrect. Although some cheats use technology, there is no mention of all defectors doing this.

B Correct. Defectors helped slaves escape and work to overthrow bad governments.

C Incorrect. While defectors innovate, it is not clear they all do.

D Incorrect. There are examples of global problems, but there is nothing about these being the goal of all defectors.

Q6

A Incorrect. The text does not say that co-operation is impossible.

B Incorrect. The increased threats are given as an example of current problems.

C Incorrect. The text doesn't mention discouraging criminals specifically.

D Incorrect. Technology is just a fact of life.

E Correct.

Q7 widespread co-operation/cooperation
Q8 expected
Q9 organizations and systems
Q10 cheating

Tips

1 Be careful: sometimes you are given words in a box to complete a summary. The words in the box might be different from in the text. They could be a different form of the same word, or synonyms, or a paraphrase (see page 51).
2 Identify the relevant section in the text, then read it carefully.
3 Remember, the information may not be in the same sequence.
4 Check the gap and predict what sort of word is needed.
5 Make sure you know how many words are required in the answer.
6 Read your completed answer and check it makes sense.

7 Re-read the text and find ten useful expressions to write in your vocabulary book. Explain to your friend why you have chosen these expressions and why you think they are useful.

Spotlight on language

Forms with *–ing*

1 For each of the sentences below, decide whether the clause with the *–ing* form:

a gives an explanation or reason
b lists a sequence of activities
c provides a description.

1 **Coming** from a small family, I am more comfortable in small groups.
2 **Having** been unemployed myself, I know how soul-destroying the experience can be.
3 **Having** completed his military training, he went on to become an officer in the army.
4 Never **having** lived in anything but a small village, she found city life overwhelming at first.
5 **Expecting** the house to be empty, the burglar broke the window and went in.
6 **Shouting** and **screaming**, the crowd started to run at the police cordon.
7 Directly on **arriving** in the country, they applied for refugee status.
8 **Having** no qualifications, they had no illusions about the sorts of jobs they could find.
9 **Sleeping** where they can, **begging** and even **stealing** if necessary, the homeless live from day to day on the margins of society.
10 He decided to make a formal complaint, **having** been treated unfairly – in his opinion – by his immediate superiors.

Active and passive infinitives

2 Decide whether one or both options in italics are grammatically and logically correct in these sentences.

1 There is still a lot *to do / to be done* before we can consider the situation acceptable.
2 I'm disappointed because I expected *to have finished / to be finished* before now.
3 Nobody can deny that the law on discrimination needs *to be changed / to have been changed.*
4 There is something *to be said / to be saying* for providing additional support for minority groups.
5 The report seems *to be suggesting / to have been suggested* a reduction in police presence as a calming measure in the worst affected areas.
6 It remains *to see / to be seen* whether the government measures actually improve the condition.
7 Five months after the riots, life in the inner-city areas seems *to be improving / to be improved.*
8 The authorities failed to *have been put / to put* in place the sort of safety net that could help these vulnerable people.
9 The desire *to be appreciated / to have appreciated* is so fundamental in all of us that it can almost *be considered / be considering* a human need.
10 If we want to prevent these problems developing into social unrest, we need *to be taking / to have been taking* action right now before it is too late.

Spotlight on exam skills 2

Note completion

1 Read this text and answer Questions 1–16 on page 67.

A A social problem can be defined as a condition that is considered undesirable by sufficient number of members of a specific community to constitute a group. There are, however, degrees of social problem, ranging from the relatively trivial to those that are so serious as to call into question the most important values of the society in question. On some there is likely to be consensus, while others may provoke extreme debate. Nobody could claim that social problems such as murder and traffic deaths resulting from drink driving are to be accepted as minor issues. However, it is not hard to find examples of other social problems that divide opinion. Teenagers playing loud music in a public park on finishing their school day obviously do not consider their behaviour unreasonable, but it may well be considered an extremely undesirable social condition by other groups who feel they have an equal right to enjoy the park and its facilities. Similarly, a number of non-smokers hold the view that smoking is an undesirable social condition that should be banned or restricted in all outdoor public areas.

B Nevertheless, research indicates there are factors that determine the degree to which a phenomenon comes to be perceived and accepted as a social problem. For example, the likelihood of a condition being considered a social problem is much greater if the group it affects are themselves powerful; that is, if they are figures of influence. For this reason, the problems that made life difficult for the poor tended to escape notice until they had some impact on the rich and middle-class citizens, for example when they became victims of crime. In the United States, the problem of drug abuse attracted substantially more attention once it spread from the lower-class, predominantly non-white population and began to affect the sons and daughters of the educated middle class.

C By much the same logic, if a condition has an impact on a small subsection of the population, it will more easily escape attention than when its adverse effects impact on a larger social group. Again, in the United States, the poverty of African Americans has featured much more prominently than the poverty of Native Americans. This can partly be explained by the fact that African Americans constitute a much larger group and are more visible.

D The third factor relates to the dynamics of the condition. If the number of people directly affected is seen to be increasing rapidly, public awareness will rise. For example, we become used to prevailing levels of crime, traffic congestion, atmospheric pollution and even political corruption. But should there be a sharp rise in intensity in one of these, public concern will also increase. One case of political corruption a year may be a source of concern for our institutions, but five such cases in one month will forcefully grab the public's attention.

E Also worth a mention is the role played by the mass media, which, according to many commentators, have largely and unfortunately failed in any attempt they might have made to address social problems. In fact, some would go further and state that if anything, television, radio and newspapers have actually contributed to the problems that exist and made them worse. This is to a great extent because they have reinforced the stereotypes that relate to race, class and gender rather than tackle them.

F Until the advent of the Internet, television was without doubt the primary vehicle through which society received its information and also the mirror of society in the way in which it reflected its values and expectations. Television has a vital role to play in the presentation of news and information. Consequently, what a particular station chooses to present as newsworthy will inevitably influence the way viewers interpret both their society and the world around them.

G All too often, television news programmes tend to focus on stories that present negative images of minority groups. We are bombarded on an almost daily basis with stories of minorities engaging in crimes such as robbery, murder and rape. These crimes by implication become characteristic of minorities. The success stories that could counterbalance this negativity are remarkably absent. The single mother who, despite the odds, finishes college with a good degree; the young man from the inner city who works his way up from the factory floor to hold a position of responsibility in the company – these stories rarely feature.

Questions 1–12

Complete the notes below.
*Choose no more than **TWO WORDS** from the text for each answer.*

What's a social problem?

Definition: A condition that a group views as **1** ....
Can be **2** .... or extremely serious
Consensus on drink driving and **3** ....
Loud music in a park: debatable

Factors influencing acceptance of social problems

- If people affected have power and **4** ....
  Example: **5** .... not considered a problem when it was limited to lower class.
- Size of the population it affects
  Example: poverty of **6** .... was overlooked.

Habit

We get used to problems like pollution, etc. However, **7** .... will attract attention.

8 ....
Addressing social problems unsuccessful or not attempted.
May have made problems **9** ....
Example: race, class, gender **10** .... not tackled, but **11** ....
Few examples of stories of **12** ....

Questions 13–16

The passage has seven paragraphs labelled **A–G**.
Which paragraph contains the following information?
*Write the correct letter, **A–G**.*
***NB** You may use any letter more than once.*

13 The significance of the size of the group of those affected
14 Deciding to ignore the positive
15 Disappointments about lack of influence on the problems
16 Disagreements of interpretation of social problems

2 Make a collection of sentences with *–ing* forms and infinitives when you next read an article online or in a newspaper. Make a copy of the article and cut out all infinitive and *–ing* forms (and remember to keep a copy of the original so you can check). The next day, see how many of the gaps you can remember accurately.

CLASSROOM WORKOUT

Crime and technology

- Brainstorm a list of crimes and write them on the board.
- Work in groups. Half the class discusses how technology can be partly responsible for the crimes listed. The other half discusses how technology could make a contribution to preventing the crimes. You should try to use at least 5–10 expressions from this unit.
- After five minutes, make pairs with one person from the other group. Discuss the two positions, and add further ideas.

CHECK YOURSELF

- How many different social issues can you remember being mentioned in this unit? Read the texts again to check if you were right.
- What other social issues are you aware of?

SUMMARY

In this unit, you:

- discussed a number of social issues. Which are most prevalent where you live?
- looked at collocations connected with social issues. How many have you written down in your notebook?
- looked at common patterns that organize texts. How many can you remember?
- studied different ways sentences develop into texts. How can this help you with the exam?
- studied and practised **note and summary completion questions**. What are the key things to remember about them?
- practised structures with *–ing* forms and infinitives. Which were not new for you?

Over to you

1 Ask your friends what they think the most pressing social issues are where you live.

2 Read newspapers and magazines to find out the latest news on what governments are doing to make life better for all groups in society.

3 Go online and find websites that support minority groups around the world. What action do they think is necessary to improve their situation? What can individuals do to help?

UNIT 6 The world around us

In this unit, you will:
- discuss the most pressing problems facing the environment
- study and practise **diagram labelling**
- study and practise **chart** and **flow-chart completion**.

Getting started

1

2

3

4

5

6
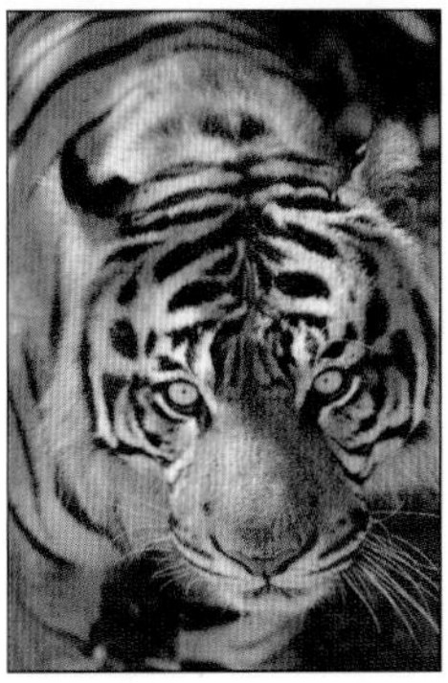

7

8

9

1 a Match the photos (1–9) with these environmental issues (a–j).

a air pollution b land use and endangered species c chemicals and toxins
d clean water e climate change f deforestation g demand for energy
h oceans and fisheries i ozone layer depletion j waste management

b Which photos could represent more than one environmental issue?

2 The environmental problems in Exercise 1 represent ten serious threats to the environment. Which do you consider to be the five most serious? Which two do you consider the least important?

3 Which of the ten environmental issues do you associate with these expressions?

floods and droughts drinkable water safe and renewable energy
endangered species pesticides and chemical compounds ultraviolet
illegal logging and cutting down the rainforest overfishing landfill
rubbish dumps smog loss of habitat the consumer society
recycling unleaded petrol acid rain polar ice caps fleet of trawlers
contamination of rivers, lakes and seas risk of disease

Spotlight on exam skills 1

Table completion

1 Match these texts (1–10) with the ten issues from page 69 (a–j).

The top 10 most serious threats facing the environment in the 21st century

1 This is an all-encompassing issue. It includes rising sea levels that threaten low-lying countries; changes in rainfall patterns that can give rise to more severe droughts in parts of Africa and around the world and floods that devastate cities, leaving thousands homeless; harsher hurricanes and other windstorms; and, worryingly, new pathways for disease.

2 For companies and countries that are big energy users, energy productivity and safe and efficient exploitation of natural resources are likely to become major strategic advantages in the future. Learning how to make better use of the finite resources of the planet is the key to our future, many claim.

3 According to some estimates, by 2030 one in three people will not have access to safe drinking water unless something is done to increase our global reserves. Rapidly developing economies and huge increases in the population of the world are putting substantial stress on this most precious resource.

4 From desertification to polar ice melting, from coastal erosion to massive deforestation, it is clear that we need to learn important lessons about effective land management very quickly. Biodiversity is a system of natural balance which preserves the food chain and the ecosystems on which all life depends. Habitat loss is a key element in the loss of biodiversity. Some scientists are open about their fears that we are in the midst of a period of mass extinction unique since the age of the dinosaurs and one that could see the disappearance of half the plant and animal species by the end of the century.

5 A significant element contributing to making all forms of pollution more dangerous is the presence of heavy metals such as lead and mercury that can poison our air, earth and water. We have no way of knowing what the long-term effects of many of these chemicals may be, as they are new. Some studies are suggesting that many compounds could be endocrine disruptors – chemicals that have a disruptive effect on the hormone balance in our body. The introduction of unleaded petrol made a significant difference, but this victory is over-shadowed by the consequences of the rapid industrial development taking place around the world. The number of people at risk of poisoning themselves by drinking polluted water, eating polluted food and using everyday objects that contain hazardous chemicals has increased alarmingly.

6 Chemicals released into the air can cause both the smog that clouds our cities and the acid rain that can devastate woodland. These and other forms of air pollution are known to contribute to chronic respiratory illnesses, which have dramatically increased over the past few decades, leading to millions of premature deaths every year. While it is true that the introduction of strict air-quality controls on factories and emissions from cars and other road-using vehicles has reduced the level of air pollution in most industrialized nations, a great deal of work remains to be done.

7 In large parts of the world, we have grown used to a throwaway lifestyle. But this is both unhealthy and unsustainable. Look at our waterways and roadsides – they are deep in the rubbish we discard. Packaging, fast food and cheap electronics are undoubtedly a significant part of the problem. In the industrialized world, so much waste is produced that we now export it to poorer countries for storage.

8 The most harmful ultraviolet radiation from the Sun is filtered out by the ozone layer before it reaches the surface of the Earth. Nevertheless, we are witnessing increased rates of skin cancer and damage to plants and ecosystems as a result of the dangerous depletion of the ozone layer. Actually, there are reasons to claim this as one of our few environmental success stories: the topic received a great deal of attention in the 1970s and '80s, when a giant 'hole' in the ozone layer was discovered above Antarctica. Luckily, people were persuaded to act quickly to scale back the production and use of CFCs and other substances proved to be responsible for the hole, so although not solved, research indicates positive signs of gradual improvement.

Tips
In these questions, you will be asked to complete gaps in a table or flow chart using a limited number of words from the text.
- Check the word limit given in the instructions and stick to it. Check whether note form is used.
- Scan the text to locate the relevant section(s) for the answers needed.
- Use the words exactly as given in the text. Don't change them.
- Check your spelling, otherwise you will lose marks.

9 With more than three-quarters of the planet covered by water, the importance of the sea is clear. Over 80 per cent of all life on Earth lives in the ocean, making it unmatched for biodiversity. Millions depend on it for their livelihood. But the vast majority of the world's fisheries are overexploited. It has been calculated that in some places, catching a ton of fish requires 17 times more effort now compared with a century ago.

10 At the current rate of destruction, the world's rainforests could have completely disappeared by the end of the century. This is serious for many reasons. The loss of habitat and resultant decline in biodiversity is just one. Deforestation also influences climate and geography and contributes to global warming. Trees are a significant part of the water cycle, and can prevent soil erosion. Agriculture is the single biggest cause of deforestation, as farmers cut forests in order to have more land for crops and animals.

2 Answer these questions.

Questions 1–8

Complete the table below.
Choose ***NO MORE THAN THREE WORDS*** *from the text for each answer.*

	Consequence	**Possible health problems**	**How the situation has developed**
Ozone layer depletion	Ultraviolet radiation no longer **1**	**2**	There has been a **3** .... in the situation.
Air pollution	Creates city smog and **4**	**5**	Pollution levels reduced following controls imposed on **6** .... and exhaust fumes from vehicles.
Chemicals and toxins	All forms of pollution are made more dangerous.	Can alter body's **7**	Millions still at risk, but use of **8** .... has been a positive contribution.

Questions 9–12

Answer the questions below using ***NO MORE THAN TWO WORDS*** *from the text for each answer.*

9 Where is the greatest biodiversity on the planet found?
10 What problem do scientists fear this age could share with the age of the dinosaurs?
11 Where is much of the industrialized world's waste sent?
12 Which professional group is most responsible for deforestation?

Tips
- Pay attention to the headings of the columns in a table so you see what information is required.
- Look at any completed examples provided for further guidance.
- Look at the gaps and predict the type of word required.

3 Find three different websites that list the most serious environmental issues facing the world today. Do the same issues still feature? Make a note of any changes.

4 Find this information on the Internet.

1 What are the ten most endangered species in the world?
2 What are the biggest cities on each continent?
3 What are the ten biggest multinational companies?
4 What are the most important measures your country has taken to protect the environment?

Vocabulary builder

Verbs of change

1 Choose the correct verbs of change in these sentences.

1 We live in a *converted* / *transformed* farmhouse. It's very modern now.
2 The book has been *turned* / *translated* into 40 languages.
3 The city centre has been completely *transformed* / *refurbished*.
4 The film paints a *blurred* / *distorted* picture of life in the US in the 1950s.
5 The two motorways *blend* / *merge* into one at the next junction.
6 Unfortunately, the problem of acid rain has *deteriorated* / *impaired* in recent years.
7 It is not easy to *amend* / *adjust* to life in a new country.
8 The hotel has *renovated* / *enhanced* all the rooms on the top floor.
9 Their parents *immigrated* / *emigrated* to Canada before they were born.
10 I asked to be *removed* / *transferred* to another office.
11 The situation is tense, and we don't want it to *escalate* / *heighten*.
12 The species that manages to *adapt* / *acclimatize* to the situation best is normally the one that survives longest.

2 Use your dictionary to find expressions with the verbs that were not the answers in Exercise 1.

3 Circle the odd one out in each list.

1 **change size:**	enlarge / grow / expand / remove
2 **change place:**	rise / relocate / transform / soar
3 **change appearance:**	dye / rejuvenate / modify / reinforce
4 **change condition:**	disguise / damage / worsen / ruin
5 **change speed:**	accelerate / embellish / rocket / rein in

4 How many different possibilities can you think of for completing these sentences logically using verbs from Exercise 3?

1 The rain .... the occasion.
2 The company .... very quickly.
3 I felt .... after the holiday.
4 We decided to .... our spending.
5 The news could .... their reputation.
6 Experiences like that can .... a person's future.
7 Prices have .... since the beginning of the year.
8 You shouldn't try to .... the truth.

5 Look back at the ten texts on pages 70–71 and find examples of verbs of change.

Most texts are to some extent about change – they talk about what has happened, is happening or may yet happen, or why these things might not or should not happen. For example, when we bring our friends and colleagues up to date in communication, whether written or spoken, we are normally informing them about some aspect of change since we last met.

Furthermore, when we communicate, we intend to add to what the listener or reader knows about a topic in some way; in other words, we hope we are changing their opinion or stock of knowledge. Consequently, you can say that most communication is concerned directly or indirectly with the topic of change.

So, when reading a text, it is a good idea to pay attention to expressions of change, as these are often key points in the overall meaning of the text.

Verbs don't generally occur on their own. Learn how verbs combine with other words. Common patterns to pay attention to are:

- verb + noun: *solve a problem, make a complaint, knock down a building, develop the city centre*
- verb + adverb: *move quickly, read aloud, change rapidly*
- verb + preposition: *turn into, pay back, drive along, rely on*
- verb + adjective: *remain calm, turn black, go cold, grow old, sound nice*

You'll find good dictionaries provide a lot of information about such verb patterns. Keep a note of the verb patterns you notice. When reading, pay attention to what the verb combines with in each sentence.

Processes

6 Complete the missing information in this table.

verb	process noun	adjective	related noun(s)
mechanize	mechanization	mechanical	mechanic
purify	**1**	pure	purity
2	colonization	colonial	colony
classify	classification	**3**	class
magnify	magnification	magnified	magnitude
4	justification	**5**	
homogenize	homogenization	**6**	homogeneity
7	hospitalization	hospitalized	hospital
minimize	minimization	minimal	**8** ....
clarify	**9**	clarified	clarity
automate	automation	**10**	automaton
simplify	simplification	simplified	**11** ....
12	computerization	**13**	computer

7 Complete these sentences using words from the table in Exercise 6.

1 The process of .... removes impurities from liquids such as milk.
2 Most office procedures have been .... – so when the computers crash, we have a problem.
3 There is little .... for behaving in that unprofessional manner.
4 This diagram was produced in order to .... the relationship between the different sections.
5 The garden was invaded by a .... of ants.
6 The teacher gave the elementary students a .... version of the book to read.
7 This product resists .... as it really is unique.
8 The problem can be solved with .... effort.

Spotlight on exam skills 2

Flow-chart completion

You should spend 20 minutes on this question.

Reverse osmosis

Our blue planet is a paradox. Life depends on water, yet in its natural form, the water in the oceans will not sustain us because we cannot drink salt water. Fortunately, salt water can be made into fresh water, with the salt removed in the process of desalination. Although historical research shows this is nothing new, it is only in the last few decades that the conversion of salt water on a large scale has become possible, though it still only accounts for a tiny proportion of our needs.

Desalination is being adopted as a solution to the problem of the scarcity of usable fresh water in areas where demand has outstripped the sustainable supply, or where natural sources of water supply are either fragile or in danger of being exhausted and also where climate change is making previously reliable sources unreliable. It takes sea water and produces water that is suitable for human consumption or for agricultural purposes by a separation process that removes the dissolved salts and other impurities. There are various methods for doing this; the one most commonly used is called reverse osmosis, which involves four major processes, or stages, namely initial pre-treatment, pressurization, membrane separation and finally post-treatment stabilization.

Once the water has been collected from its source, it is transported to a holding basin. In reverse osmosis, pre-treatment is very important, as the surfaces of the membranes that play a central role in this method of desalination need to remain clean to work effectively and can be easily dirtied and damaged by impurities in the feed water, as it is now called. In the initial part of this pre-treatment stage, pieces of wood and smaller suspended solids like sand are removed by passing the feed water through a particle filter. Then the filtered water is pumped through fine carbon microfilters that trap minerals and contaminants such as pesticides. Chlorine is also removed here as a protective measure, as it would otherwise shorten the life of the membranes. Next, the water is put under high pressure and pushed through the permeable membranes arranged in series, which prevent the passage of dissolved salts in the seawater, while allowing the separated and desalinated product water to pass through. Approximately half the feedwater becomes product water. The remaining 50%, now with a higher concentration of salts, is rejected and returned to the source. In the post-treatment stage, the product water undergoes blending with chemicals and minerals. Finally, the product water is sent to a cistern, where it is stored awaiting distribution for use.

Reverse osmosis is growing in popularity, as major improvements in the membranes, energy recovery, pumps and pressure vessels over the past ten to 20 years have brought down the cost of desalinated water significantly.

Questions 1–7

Complete the flow chart below.
Choose ***NO MORE THAN TWO WORDS*** *from the text for each answer.*

The desalination of sea water by reverse osmosis

Seawater collected from ocean and sent to **1** ....

↓

Initial pre-treatment stage uses **2** .... to ensure removal of solids.
Removal of **3** .... also important in order to protect membrane.

↓

Water pumped at **4** .... through series of membranes.
5 .... are removed here, and separation is completed.

↓

Rejected water is sent back to **6** ....

↓

In post-treatment stage, **7** .... with chemicals and minerals takes place. Then the product water can be sent to storage.

Questions 8–10

Which ***THREE*** *of the following facts about the process of desalination are mentioned in the text?*

A It is cheaper now than it was in previous years.
B It is more energy efficient than other methods.
C Its end product is not restricted to use as drinking water.
D It returns water back to the source in an altered condition.
E It involves the use of dangerous chemicals.

Spotlight on language

Conditional practice

1 Complete the sentences below with the words and expressions in the box.

as long as	if exploitation	if that were not the case
if the situation is to change	If we continue	if we didn't use them
if we look back	if we want to	if you are poor
otherwise	unless something	whether or not

1 a We exploit the natural resources of the planet because there is really no other choice .... enjoy the quality of life we have.

b The resources are there to be exploited, and .... , we would have to make serious changes to our lifestyles.

c .... of the planet's resources continues as at present, then the lifestyle we currently enjoy runs the risk of causing significant damage to the world.

2 a .... is done about it, the rising sea levels we have already witnessed will threaten many low-lying countries.

b Low-lying countries like Holland and many Pacific islands can survive .... further measures are taken to protect their coastlines from erosion and the threat posed by the sea.

c The future of many countries depends on .... we can find an effective solution to the challenge represented by the continued and accelerating melting of polar ice sheets and the resultant change in sea level.

3 a We live in a world of inequalities, and as far as poverty is concerned, it has long been recognized that .... , the key must lie in ensuring children in poor families have access to education.

b The value of education as a positive force for society has been largely taken for granted by the middle classes, who benefit from it in great numbers, whereas in many parts of the world, ... , you tend to face the stark choice between education or sending your children out in search of any type of work that can put food on the table.

c It is not that people question whether education can help lift the poor out of the poverty that is their prison, but rather that the day-to-day reality for people in that situation is that they must do what they have to in order to survive. .... , there would be no child labour, something the middle classes sometimes fail to comprehend.

4 a In this time of accelerating change in all aspects of life, it is often forgotten that ecosystems are undergoing a process of constant change and are themselves subject to evolution, so that at various times they will be composed of different organisms. .... at the ecosystems of 10,000 years ago, they are different from the ones we have today.

b As we continue to lose species at a rapid rate, it is imperative that we discover which losses will have the most serious consequences on ecosystems, ... the unprecedented degree of change risks causing the collapse of the ecosystems that we all ultimately depend on.

c .... to lose species at the same alarming rate as at present, there is no doubt that the ecosystems will be profoundly different by the end of the century; however, we must also remember that the process of loss through evolution is a natural one and not unique to this day and age.

2 In each group of three sentences in Exercise 1, at least two of them have more or less the same meaning. It is possible that all three are similar in meaning. Read the sentences in each group and decide which one, if any, is the odd one out, and say why.

Sentence completion

3 Complete these sentences so they are true for you.

1 As long as I work hard, I should ...
2 Having a good level of English is important, otherwise ...
3 I want to get a good result in the IELTS test. If that were not the case, ...
4 My plans for the future depend on whether or not ...
5 If I continue to develop my vocabulary and practise my pronunciation, ...
6 If I look back on the past year, the things that have been most important for me ...
7 Unless something unexpected happens, I will ...
8 If people like me want to make a big difference to the world, we ...
9 I think if people want to tackle the problems of the environment, we ...
10 If I want to fulfil my ambitions and make my dreams come true, I ...

Useful expressions with *if* ...

4 How many of these expressions do you know how to use? Check in a good dictionary.

if I were you
if necessary
if it comes to that
if you ask me
if at all
so what if
if and when
if anything
if it's all the same to you
if you don't mind
if only

5 Which of the expressions in Exercise 4 best completes each of these sentences?

1 The current situation is difficult, with some economies growing by less than 1%, ...
2 You asked me for my advice. Well, ... , I would walk a bit more rather than taking a taxi everywhere. It's good for you and the environment.
3 It's depressing talking about the problems facing the environment. .... , I'd rather change the subject.
4 I don't think governments should be content with what they are doing to value and protect wildlife. .... , they should do more.
5 Fish stocks are dangerously low. Overfishing might drive some species to extinction. .... , we will have destroyed the balance of life in our oceans for ever.
6 We know now that we made serious mistakes in the past. .... we could turn back time!
7 The protesters were prepared to go to prison for what they believed in ....
8 I just don't believe global warming is a proven fact. .... it rains a bit more in some parts of the world? It's not my problem.

Spotlight on exam skills 3

Table completion

In this question type, you fill in the gaps in a table using words from the text. You will be told the maximum number of words you can use – often three. Do not use any other words and make sure the words you do use are spelled correctly.

1 Read this text, then answer Questions 1–8 on page 79.

Extremophiles – living life on the edge.

You may think that people are capable of living in a wide range of environments, from the hot deserts of Africa and the Middle East to the freezing cold of Siberia or Northern Canada. Being an intelligent species, we worked out how to use fire to keep us warm in cold conditions and, considerably later, air conditioning to keep us cool in hot climates. But our ability to survive in extreme conditions is surpassed by a wide variety of organisms capable of thriving in environments in which no human could survive – the extremophiles.

Take, for example, *Spinoloricus cinzia*, a tiny creature, about a millimetre long and looking a little like a jellyfish. This recently discovered animal is particularly interesting, as it appears to be capable of living without oxygen and is thus a multi-cellular anaerobe. The cells of most organisms contain mitochondria, which use oxygen to generate energy, whereas the cells of *Spinoloricus cinzia* do not contain mitochondria. Most anaerobes so far discovered are microbes and use a form of fermentation to gain energy – such as those found in human intestines. Some anaerobes will actually die in the presence of oxygen.

In some parts of the world, there are deep-sea hydrothermal vents through which very hot water flows into the sea. Recent studies have shown that there are some thermophilic bacteria, such as *Methanopyrus kandleri*, which are capable of surviving near these vents – in temperatures of up to 120 degrees Celsius – and they may in fact die in temperatures below 50 degrees Celsius. The important factor that allows such organisms to survive at such temperatures is the presence of enzymes that can withstand intense heat – heat that would destroy the enzymes found in other organisms.

While there are many examples of small creatures such as bacteria that are extremophiles, there are others, such as *Pachycereus pringlei*, which are almost 20 metres tall. *Pachycereus pringlei* is a cactus which grows in north-western Mexico and is a member of the class of xerophiles, organisms that are capable of surviving in an environment with very little water. Xerophilic organisms have adapted to such environments; for example, a saguaro cactus can absorb 760 litres of water during a rainstorm. Another adaptation is a long taproot, which can be several times longer than the part of the plant above ground.

You may not be familiar with *Helicobacter pylori*, but there is a good chance you are carrying around a few million of them in your stomach, as more than half the people in the world have them. *Helicobacter pylori* are a kind of bacteria which are able to survive inside your stomach, where the environment is strongly acidic. It can do this by having a thick cell membrane and also by producing a chemical called ammonium, which neutralizes the acids found in the stomach.

While most acidophilic organisms find strategies for surviving in acid environments by neutralizing the acid, one acidophile, *Acetobacter aceti*, positively thrives in an acid environment. This bacteria has special proteins which can survive in very acid environments, so there is no need for it to modify the acidity.

While extremophiles might be seen as an interesting novelty, some of them play an important role in industrial processes. For example, many anaerobic bacteria are used in the production of biogas from cattle manure. Thermophilic bacteria are being used to remove toxic chemicals from soils and sediments. With the unstable nature of world weather patterns, xerophilic plants could prove useful in agriculture. The acidophilic *Acetobacter aceti* is already extensively used in the food industry. This tiny microbe is capable of turning ethanol into vinegar.

Questions 1–8

Complete the chart below.
Choose ***NO MORE THAN TWO WORDS*** *from the text for each answer.*

Kind of organism	Description of environment in which it lives	How the organism has adapted	Example of how the organism can benefit humans
anaerobes	An environment in which there is no **1**	Uses **2** .... to produce energy	Able to produce **3** .... from animal waste
thermophiles	Hot areas with a temperature between 50 and 120 degrees Celsius	Has special **4** .... that do not break down in high temperatures	Able to break down **5** .... in earth
6	Areas with very little water	The ability to **7** .... water quickly	May have an increased role in agriculture
acidophiles	Areas where the pH is very low	Able to neutralize acids or to withstand acid conditions	Important microbes in the production of **8** ....

Expressions with *earth*

2 Use the context of these sentences to work out what the expressions in italics mean. Check your answers in a good dictionary.

1 Why *on earth* did you do that?
2 He said he's the happiest man *on earth* at the moment.
3 Then he made an *earth-shattering* discovery.
4 There's *no earthly reason* for reacting like that.
5 Good holidays needn't *cost the earth.*
6 Returning to work after the holiday always brings me *back down to earth with a bump.*
7 The poor live in simple shacks with *earthen* floors.
8 My favourite subject at school was *earth sciences.*
9 He's got a very *earthy* manner, and not everybody likes that.
10 They don't have much money, but people like them are the *salt of the earth.*
11 It was as if they had vanished *off the face of the earth.*

CLASSROOM WORKOUT

Crosswords

- Work in pairs. Each pair draws a crossword grid (suggested size is 12×12) and makes a crossword puzzle using the environmental problems mentioned in this unit and the expressions with *earth* from Exercise 2 on page 79. The answers should be a mixture of nouns, verbs and adjectives. Write the clues for your answers, then swap crossword puzzles with another pair.
- Which pair is quickest to solve the puzzle?

CHECK YOURSELF

- Make a list of 10–15 verbs you could use to discuss changes involved in the different processes mentioned in this unit.
- Write down five facts you know about the importance of water as a result of reading the texts in this unit.

SUMMARY

In this unit, you:

- discussed a number of challenges facing the environment. What are the five most serious, in your opinion?
- looked at verbs of change. How many have you written down in your notebook?
- completed a chart with vocabulary about processes. How many words did you know?
- practised **flow-chart completion**. What are the key points to remember?
- practised **table completion**. Can you change the words you find in the text?
- practised conditional structures. Which were not new for you?
- did some paraphrase practice identifying similarities and differences between short texts. Why is it important to be able to spot paraphrases in the exam?

Over to you

1 Make a collection of expressions with *if*, *unless*, *otherwise* and *whether* and try to use at least one every day.
2 Read newspapers and magazines to find articles about business, scientific, economic and natural processes.
3 Go online and find websites that tackle environmental issues. Read them and evaluate how convincing their arguments are. Pay attention to the verbs of change they use in their texts.

UNIT 7 Sell, sell, sell

In this unit, you will:
- discuss advertising
- study and practise **True / False / Not Given** tasks
- learn collocations about marketing.

Getting started

1 Look at these three photos and decide what could be the most effective way of advertising each product. What features of each product would you want to stress?

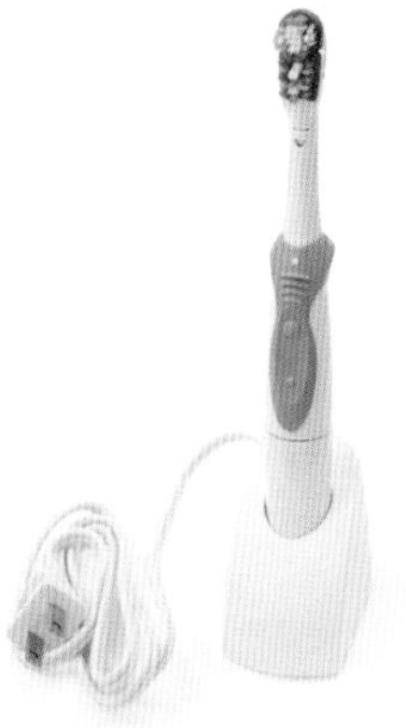

2 Complete the table below with these phrases.

time-saving   low-cost   high in protein   great taste   precision-engineered
healthy gums   long-lasting smile   money-saving   low fat   labour-saving
for whiter teeth   high-performance   environmental impact   good for you

electric toothbrush	hybrid car	milk

3 In your opinion, which of these forms of advertising would be most suitable for the three different products?

1 TV advertising
2 billboards
3 telephone marketing
4 social media
5 free samples
6 newspaper ads
7 radio ads
8 trade fairs
9 bulk mailing
10 email

Vocabulary builder 1

Advertising

1 Read the short texts below and on page 83 (A–F) and decide if these statements are True (T), False (F) or Not Given (NG).

1 Everyone has a favourite form of advertising, but the most annoying is generally acknowledged to be full-page advertising in newspapers and glossy magazines.
2 Companies must be able to give evidence that the claims made in their advertising are true.
3 The amount of advertising we are subject to has increased dramatically in recent years as a result of social media and email, with its daily dose of unwanted spam messages.
4 Special techniques are employed to make sure products appeal to children.
5 It is easier to advertise cheaper products such as educational toys than more expensive items like hybrid cars.
6 There is growing public concern about the influence advertising may have on certain groups of people.
7 Customers buy products in the clear belief that the benefits of the products advertised are truthful.
8 The aim of all advertising and promotional material is to persuade people to take a course of action, which is usually to purchase the product or service in question.
9 It is generally accepted that all adverts aim to create clear messages that are quick and easy to understand.

A

A company that produces baby milk has been criticized by the advertising watchdog for making a number of claims that were ruled to be misleading and not supported by robust evidence. The company said it accepted the ruling in its entirety.

B

An unsatisfied customer is taking Honda to court for what she alleges are the shortcomings of her hybrid car. Having originally made the purchase of the car in the expectation of saving money at the petrol pump, she claims the car fails to deliver the 51-miles-per-gallon performance advertised.

C

Following years of increasingly vociferous complaints from educational bodies, parents, church groups and others, the government is to launch an official inquiry into the possible harmful effects of advertising on children. It plans to investigate evidence of connections between adverts and anxiety, eating disorders and drinking.

D

The advertising of toys is aimed at two distinct groups. When advertising to children, the emphasis is placed on fun and excitement, an effect achieved by the focus on bright colours, fast-moving images and the association with famous TV characters. The use of large boxes in packaging enhances this attractiveness. When advertising to adults, however, it is the educational benefits that are promoted.

E

In a series of studies designed to analyze consumer reactions to advertising claims, scientists found that ambiguous descriptions tend to be interpreted in two different ways. Consumers either infer that the attributes refer to technical details that are likely to be informative to people who are more knowledgeable than they are, or they assume that the purpose of the description is simply to sound persuasive.

F

When asked about attitudes towards different forms of advertising, consumers rated interruptive or intrusive formats such as telemarketing and spam email as most annoying, and print advertising in newspapers or magazines and outdoor advertising were rated most positively, although nobody is likely to confess to wanting more advertising in their lives.

2 Find and underline at least ten expressions relating to advertising in the texts above.

3 Match the two halves of these marketing collocations, then match them with their definitions (a–i).

Example: 1 trade mark, c

1 trade	revenue
2 sales	reputation
3 product	loyalty
4 exclusive	research
5 good	agreement
6 market	mark
7 brand	launch
8 franchise	endorsement
9 celebrity	rights

a when something new is brought to the market
b when no one else is allowed to provide the same service
~~**c** a name or symbol which identifies a product~~
d when people think highly of a person or company
e customers sticking to favourite products
f an arrangement with a parent company to run a related business
g the money that is generated
h surveys to find out if there is a demand for a service in an area
i the use of the famous to promote a product

Spotlight on exam skills 1

True / False / Not Given

In this question type, you need to decide whether a statement is true, false or not given **in the text**.

Tips

1. Scan the text to find the relevant paragraph.
2. Look for text which supports the statement, though don't expect to see exactly the same words.
3. Look out for anything to show that the statement is not true, and pay particular attention to verbs that contradict or negate a sentence, such as *deny, refuse, criticize.*
4. When you have scanned the text and located the relevant place in the text, if there is no information, then the answer is 'Not Given'.
5. The questions follow the order of the text.
6. You must only base your answer on the information in the text, not on what you may know. If the information is true but not written in the text, the answer is 'Not Given'.
7. Also pay attention to comparative structures, and to words and expressions that qualify a statement, such as *mainly, always, often, never* or verbs that have different degrees of truth, such as *suggest, claim, believe, know.*
8. Just write 'True', 'False' or 'Not Given'. No further information is required.
9. Remember, there will be at least one of each type of answer.

1 Read this text and decide whether the statements below are True (T), False (F) or Not Given (NG). Pay attention to the underlined words in the questions.

You've got mail – and LOTS of it!

It has been estimated that an astonishing 71% of all mail addressed to you – direct mail – is junk mail. This is all mail looking for business from you. You are a potential customer, and someone, somewhere is hoping you will buy, or at least respond to, some compelling offer. That's annoying enough, but add to that figure all the unsolicited generic – hence indirect – mail that is shoved through your letterbox without your name on it, and you have a figure of truly staggering proportions. To that can be added all the advertising material inserted inside every newspaper or magazine you pick up, generally in effect doubling their size, which is a specific problem with the format. Statistics are hard to come by, rather like a closely guarded secret; however, some calculate that at least 3.4 billion items of direct mail and 13 billion items of unaddressed mail such as inserts and flyers were sent out in 2005 in the UK alone. While the environmental impact of such use of paper is clearly significant, the sheer volume of the issue – which is similar in every developed country in the world – is an indication that there is something in it for businesses, otherwise they simply wouldn't engage in such a costly and labour-intensive activity.

1. It is <u>not always</u> clear what the purpose of direct mail is.
2. There is <u>more</u> direct mail in the UK <u>than elsewhere</u> in the world.
3. <u>Most</u> people receive <u>more</u> direct mail than indirect mail.
4. The author has a <u>negative</u> opinion of junk mail.
5. Newspapers and magazines <u>often</u> carry additional advertising.
6. The <u>true</u> figures for the amount of direct and indirect mail sent out cannot be calculated.
7. <u>Every year</u>, people in the UK receive about 13 billion items of indirect mail.
8. Businesses invest in these forms of advertising because they are profitable.

Comments
1 False: *This is all mail looking for business from you.*
2 Not Given: There is no mention of other countries.
3 Not Given: The passage does not compare the quantities of both types of mail.
4 True: *That's annoying enough ...*
5 True: *... inserted inside every newspaper or magzine you pick up ...*
6 True: *Statistics are hard to come by ... some calculate that at least ...*
7 False: This is the figure for 2005.
8 True: *... there is something in it for businesses ...*

2 Re-read the two sentences in the right-hand column of the text on page 84 (*Statistics ... activity.*) and try to write three statements for each sentence: one that would produce a True answer, one a False answer and one a Not Given answer. Which is the easiest/hardest to write?

Vocabulary builder 2

Lifestyle

1 Complete the sentences below with the words in the box. There is one word you will not need.

addiction	affluent	ego
eye-catching	lifestyle	shopaholic

1 It can't be easy being a top football manager, as the players almost all have a fragile .... that the manager has to cope with.
2 It was not long ago that mobile phones were only used by the most .... members of society, with everyone else using public phones and landlines.
3 Should you wear .... clothes for an interview, or is it better that your personality is what they remember?
4 In the past, many people connected the word '............................' with things like drugs, but nowadays, people realize that work can also fall into the same category.
5 Would you like to lead a jet-setting .... , or would you prefer to stay in one place with your close family and friends?

2 Which word did you not use in Exercise 1? Are you one? What are the symptoms of being one? Is it a serious problem or a bit of a joke?

Collocation practice

3 Complete these collocations from the text on page 84 without re-reading it.

1 junk ....
2 shove ....
3 staggering ....
4 advertising ....
5 hard to ....
6 a .... guarded secret
7 the .... impact
8 the .... volume
9 in every .... country
10 there's something .... for

4 Complete the missing prepositions in these expressions from the same text.

1 mail addressed .... you
2 looking .... business from
3 without your name .... it
4 engage .... such a costly activity

Spotlight on exam skills 2

True / False / Not Given

1 Read this text carefully.

Shopping for what we need or what we want?

Over the past hundred years, shopping has grown to become one of the leading pastimes of an increasing proportion of populations in rich and developing nations alike. Indeed, for many – and this is not necessarily restricted to the most affluent – shopping is cited as the number-one hobby. Changes in modern lifestyles mean that for many families, it is no longer eating together but shopping that bonds them as a family, at least at the weekend. The era that invented the term 'shopaholic' witnessed shopping, originally the necessary process of exchanging goods or services in order to eat and dress, become acknowledged as a serious addiction if not by all branches of medicine, at least by the general public, and as such, it is an issue that merits serious study.

One reason for this lies in how the products we shop for are marketed. It is not simply a case of presenting the public with a product in an eye-catching manner. Advertising works by focusing on the promotion of our ego, the sense of ourselves that we identify with, rather than on specific objective facts of whatever it is we buy. The 'feel-good factor' often associated with purchasing items can be explained in these terms rather than price or value, although of course everyone likes to feel that he or she has got a bargain. Companies know that they don't sell products, they sell us lifestyles, regardless of whether they are selling a cheap daily necessity or a special luxury item: everything from our breakfast cereals to the cars we drive is marketed in this way. We buy a toothbrush or a pair of jeans and we actually buy into an image of ourselves that is defined by what we have, not who we are.

2 Look at the underlined phrases in the text and the expressions in bold in these statements, then decide if the statements are True (T), False (F) or Not Given (NG).

1. Shopping has **only recently** become a social pleasure.
2. The interest in shopping as a way of spending time crosses **social and national** borders.
3. In **most** families, shared mealtimes have been replaced by shopping as an opportunity for family togetherness.
4. **Medical research** is being conducted into the problem of excessive shopping.
5. The success of an advert relies **on more than** the nature and properties of the product itself.
6. The act of buying something creates a sense of satisfaction, **as long as** the buyer has got value for money.
7. **It is easier** to sell cheaper products than more expensive items because they don't rely on sophisticated sales techniques.
8. Our possessions **make statements about** our identity.

Comments

1 False: The first line talks about *over the past 100 years*, which cannot be considered 'only recently'.
2 True: The text refers to rich and poor people, and in rich and developing nations.
3 False: There is a difference between *many* and *most families*. The qualifier *at least at the weekend* also makes the generalization false.
4 Not Given: Although there is mention of the phenomenon being acknowledged by some branches of medicine and that further study is merited, there is no mention that research is being carried out. This does not mean that research *isn't* being carried out, simply that such research is not mentioned in the text.
5 True: There is reference to adverts promoting the feel-good factor and lifestyle which are not connected to the nature and properties of the product itself.
6 False: While it is true that many people like to get a bargain, a sense of satisfaction can be achieved by other means, such as the feel-good factor.
7 Not Given: Expensive and inexpensive goods are mentioned, but it is not discussed whether cheaper goods are easier to sell. Although this may be the case, as it is not stated in the text, the answer has to be 'Not Given'.
8 True: As stated in the last sentence of the text.

3 Read this text, then decide whether the questions on page 88 are True (T), False (F) or Not Given (NG).

The development of market research

There have been considerable improvements to the way products and services are marketed over the years. Much of this can be attributed to the creation of market research as an industry, which saw its beginnings in the latter part of the 1920s in the United States with the work of a man named Daniel Starch.

The common practice at that time was for copywriters to think up an appropriate and perhaps catchy text to attract the attention of the buying public, publish the ad, and then hope that readers would act upon the information provided and buy the product or service.

During the early 1930s, Daniel Starch developed the theory that in order to be effective, advertising must be seen, read, believed, remembered and then acted upon. He went on to develop a research company that would stop people going about their business in the streets, asking them if they read certain publications. If they did, his researchers would show them the magazines and ask if they recognized or remembered any of the ads found in them. Having collected the data, he then compared the number of people he interviewed with the circulation of the magazine to calculate how effective those ads were in reaching their readers. Thus surveying or 'market research' was born.

As time went on, many more market-research companies began to emerge and followed Starch's example. It was not long before they were working to improve on his techniques. George Gallup, whose name is now associated with opinion polls, developed a rival system that was known as 'aided recall', which prompted those interviewed to recall the ads seen in a publication, without actually showing them the ads. This rival system was later adopted by companies to measure the effectiveness of radio and television advertising.

In the late 1980s, Ronald Lindorf founded what would be one of the largest market-research companies in the United States, Western Wats. The focus of Western Wats was to leverage the current technology of

WATS telephone lines to conduct survey research. There was no longer a need to interview people on the streets or to organize and conduct focus groups. A representative in a call center could collect all of the data desired. This greatly increased the number of surveys collected each year and improved the market-research model ten-fold.

Over the last five to ten years, market research has taken another great leap forward in terms of methods of data collection. While surveys are still employed, this is largely done via internet connection. Western Wats (recently renamed as Opinionology) is still the largest market-research company in the US and collects the majority of their research via their online panel called Opinion Outpost. Rather than cold-calling an individual in the search for data, the company has online studies that anyone interested in participating in can sign up to receive and freely share their opinion. It is much less intrusive, and the quality of data is often much higher, since people can participate on their own schedule, instead of being rushed when they receive a phone call from a call center.

This use of internet technology shows how far the quest to gather public opinion has come since the 1820s, when it is said that the first recorded straw polls – the term comes from farmers throwing a handful of straw into the air to check which direction the wind was coming from – were recorded. Nowadays, it seems that everyone from political parties to companies marketing toothbrushes wants to see which way the wind of public opinion is blowing before making a decision.

adapted from www.marketresearchworld.net

1 Market research was developed when Daniel Starch was employed to see how effective and memorable advertising was.
2 Methods considered appropriate for researching the effectiveness of radio and television advertising differed from those used by Starch.
3 Western Wats introduced methods generally considered less efficient than those of Starch and Gallup.
4 The rebranding of Western Wats as Opinionology resulted in the creation of the biggest market-research company in the world.
5 There had been no interest in finding public opinion before the market-research industries began their work in the last century.

4 Think of two different ways of expressing the same meaning as these phrases from the text above.

1 There have been considerable improvements ...
2 The common practice at that time ...
3 ... act upon the information provided ...
4 As time went on, ...
5 It was not long before ...

Spotlight on language

Paraphrase practice

1 Explain the difference between each of these words or expressions.

1 process / procedure / production line
2 job / career / profession / business
3 launch your product / promote your product / stock your product
4 sell by / sell out / sell for
5 earn / deserve / be worth
6 man management / middle management / micro-management
7 acknowledge / admit / agree
8 claim / state / allege

2 Complete these sentences with words or expressions from Exercise 1.

1 In big companies like ours, we have lots of systems in place. In fact, we have a .... for everything, from ordering stationery to asking for paternity leave. In fact, I'm in the .... of writing new guidelines for using the car park.
2 Leaving his last company proved to be a good .... move for Kim. Within two years, he was managing a department. Not long after that, ... really took off and soon he had a place on the Board.
3 You may have had the best product in the world on the market for ages, but if you don't know how to .... , then you are unlikely to succeed, as shops will not be willing to ....
4 Supermarket managers are like jugglers. They have many products that have a .... date, and money is wasted if they are not sold promptly. Also, if they .... of a particular product, they will have to deal with some irate customers.
5 It's a sad fact of life that you don't always get what you .... However, it's also true that when you .... something by the fruits of your own labour, you appreciate it more than if you have the same thing as a gift.
6 Now that I am in .... , I am answerable to some people, and other people are answerable to me. I try to delegate wherever I can. However, when I was younger and starting out in business, the way my boss treated me was the perfect example of .... He checked everything I did, and I hated it.
7 While you may not .... with everything that big corporations do, you have to .... their success in the last 100 years.
8 He doesn't .... to have stayed within the law all his life, but he's far from being the criminal that some people ....

3 Complete these sentences logically.

1 To keep their products rolling off the production line, ...
2 The profession a lot of people want to go into ...
3 Launching a new product is often both risky and expensive because ...
4 These days, top computers sell for ...
5 In business, knowing how much something is worth ...

Spotlight on exam skills 3

True / False / Not Given

1 Read this text, then do the exam task on page 91.

How an advert is created

You may love them or loathe them, but a lot of work goes into creating the advertisements that we see, hear or read. Although they may only be 30 seconds long, or a few lines of text and a photo, there has probably been weeks if not months of work behind the production of the advertisement. But what is the process which leads to the production of an advertisement? There is no one path that all advertising agencies take, but there are some general ideas which are common to the vast majority of advertising projects.

First steps

The first stage is when the client contacts the advertising company and submits a brief, which, by definition, is not that long. It could be that a company wants to launch a new product. Thousands of new products are launched every year, but very few of them become successful and are still around ten years after their launch. The company may want to improve its market share. How many different companies are there selling cars, chocolate bars or computer services? There are only a limited number of customers, so companies are willing to spend a lot of money on increasing their share of the pie through advertising. The company may simply want to remain the market leader and realize that advertising may be the key to their success. The company could be a regular client who was satisfied with an earlier campaign or it could be a new company who has been impressed with other campaigns you have handled.

Research begins

Once the brief is in the hands of the advertising company, the research can begin which will include an analysis of the client's current products and their position in the market place. The company itself is likely to be able to provide that data, but the advertising agency may need to do further research to measure the perception of the product compared to the client's competitors and also the kind of advertising the competition is using.

Then the company will discuss a wide range of factors about the product itself: what are the demographics (age, sex, education, income levels, etc.) and location of the people who are likely to use the product? It is well known that some products sell very well in some areas but not in others. Mushy peas, for example, are very popular in the north of England, but are rarely seen on dinner plates in the south. Seasonality is another factor which can influence an advertising campaign. You don't see many adverts for lawn mowers in November, or adverts for snow clearers in June for obvious reasons. Such factors need to be considered before planning begins.

Now to the plan

Once the basic research is over, it is up to the planning team to decide how the target audience can best be reached in the most cost-effective way. They may decide on the best pricing structure for the company, perhaps offering the product at a lower price initially so that people try the products. They need to decide on which media channels will be used. Is the product something visual, so television is the best medium? Or can the product be advertised using radio advertising, which is generally much cheaper? Companies will also look at targeting the advertising: if the product is suitable for travellers, then they may have advertisements in trains and at airports. If the product is likely to sell well to sportspeople, then a poster campaign in and around sports centres might be the best way.

Another important role for the planning team is to start creating the content that will woo the potential customers and help the company's sales skyrocket. The goal of advertisers is to produce a slogan that people remember and use on a regular basis – promoting brand awareness well outside the original advertisement.

Executing the plan

The creative team will then decide exactly how the message will be presented. Will the visual material used feature a serious person in a white coat? Will it be a happy, successful looking couple? Maybe an animated character? They also need to decide whether the message will tell you how good the product is or how good you will feel when you use the product. Once the advert has been created on paper, it is usually 'farmed out' to outside production companies who will do the actual recording or filming with some people within the agency tracking the whole process so that the advertisement is produced within a certain timeframe and, very importantly, as financial penalties could otherwise be involved, within budget.

Following up

Once the advertisements have appeared on TV or in a magazine, the advertising agency follows up to make sure that the ads were shown when they were supposed to be shown and also to see how effective the campaign was. Of course, the best measure of success is when your clients return again and again, perhaps with happy tales of boosting sales volumes, as they are clearly satisfied with your work.

So next time you hear, read or listen to an advertisement, spend a moment or two considering all the work which went into producing it.

Questions 1–5

Do the following statements agree with the information given in the passage?

Write

TRUE *if the statement agrees with the information*
FALSE *if the statement contradicts the information*
NOT GIVEN *if there is no information on this*

1 Many products enter the market, but few of them survive longer than a decade.
2 There are more companies selling computer services than cars.
3 Location of likely customers is one factor that can affect how an advertising campaign is organised.
4 Radio advertising is much cheaper than advertising through magazines and newspapers.
5 Advertising agencies usually carry out all the work themselves, from research, planning and creating the final film, rather than using the expertise of other companies.

Questions 6–12

Complete the following table with **NO MORE THAN THREE WORDS** *from the text.*

Step 1: initial phase	A **6** .... is given to the advertising agency.	
Step 2: research	It is necessary to produce **7** .... of how the company is doing compared to its competitors.	Age, sex and education of the potential customers are just three of a **8** .... that need to be considered by the company.
Step 3: planning	No company wants to pay too much, so the advertising company must look for a campaign that is the most **9** .... for their client.	People tend to buy products they are familiar with, so **10** .... is a vital part of an advertising strategy.
Step 4: execution	Some companies are fined if they don't stay **11** .... when carrying out a project.	
Step 5: follow-up	Increased sales is just one **12** .... for a company. Employee and customer satisfaction are other important ones.	

Vocabulary development

2 a Complete these useful expressions and collocations from the text on page 90.

How an advert is created
1 love them or .... them
2 a lot of work .... into
3 the .... majority

First steps
4 few are still .... ten years after (their launch)
5 improve its market ....
6 a limited .... of
7 the .... to their success

b Now find more useful expressions and collocations from the other sections of the text.

CLASSROOM WORKOUT

The art of persuasion.

- Work in small groups. Choose one item that you have with you, for example a watch, a phone, a book.
- Think of the positive qualities of that item and prepare a short presentation for the other groups to convince them that they should buy that item. Try to use some of the language that you have seen in this unit.
- Which group can make the most convincing presentation?

CHECK YOURSELF

- Look back through the unit and make a collection of ideas and expressions which are a) positive of and b) critical about advertising.
- Draw a table and summarize the ideas in two columns.

SUMMARY

In this unit, you:

- looked at various forms of advertising. Which forms of advertising do you find most effective, and why ?
- studied many collocations connected with marketing. Were any of them new to you?
- looked at **True / False / Not Given** questions. What errors do some students make with this particular question form?
- did a **table completion** exercise. Do you feel comfortable with this question form now?
- read about the history and methods of market research. What did you learn?
- collected useful expressions from the passages. Which are most useful?

Over to you

- Go online and compare the websites of three different advertising agencies. What products or services do they advertise? Which seems the most creative?
- Find the website of an official body that checks adverts (such as the Advertising Standards Agency, www.asa.org.uk). Find out what they do, what resources they have on their website, and what the advertising codes are.

UNIT 8 The road to success

In this unit, you will:
- discuss success and failure
- study and practise **Yes / No / Not Given** tasks
- look at patterns in a text.

Getting started

1 These photos show different aspects of success. Think about what kinds of success these people might have achieved, and which is the most important to you.

2 What role might be played by each of these aspects in the successes in Exercise 1?

luck talent hard work determination money support and encouragement opportunity

Spotlight on exam skills 1

Yes / No / Not Given

Read the text below and on page 94. Are the answers to these statements 'Yes', 'No' or 'Not Given'?

According to the writer ...

1 anyone can be successful at school if they set the right targets.
2 all forms of success depend on hard work.
3 everyone has some sort of ambition.
4 success in sport often depends on making sacrifices.
5 the financial rewards compensate for the fact that sporting careers are short.
6 many people fail to understand one of the key elements of business success.

The nature of success

We live in a world where success is highly valued in all fields of endeavour. However, is it really possible to compare success in business or sports with success in the academic world of studies? Success at school comes from a certain amount of application and certainly is not given to everyone, although nobody actually aims to do badly in exams. But what does it lead to? The correlation between good exam results as a teenager and a good degree and success beyond one's studies is hard to measure. This is perhaps because school and university are seen as steps towards something further and not a goal in their own right. Success in exams, you might say, is like winning part of a race, but not the race itself. Despite the high expectations that they might have had, the reality is that millions of graduates across the world are in jobs that do not stretch them, or are not particularly well-rewarded; many recent graduates are unable to even find a job of any sort in these times of economic uncertainty. In other words, academic success seems to be an unreliable indicator of actual potential.

Sporting success brings local, national or international acclaim, and, in the case of the most popular professional sports, financial rewards that are beyond the reach of most of us. What do most successful sports men and women have in common? Natural ability and a great deal of training, for sure. Many will have decided to turn their backs on the parties and socializing of their peers in order to do more lengths in the pool or more hours in the gym, to work on their sprint or serving or cycling or passing techniques. Another sad fact of sporting life is that careers are short and often plagued by injury.

In business, success is generally measured by salary rather than specific achievements, records or popularity. When asked, most people who have fulfilled their ambitions in business will attribute their success to putting in long hours in the early stages of their career, and determination. In addition, however, they will almost always mention something that is all too often overlooked by those for whom business is simply a way of paying the bills, and that's innovation. Business success does not come to those who simply do their jobs or follow their leaders. It is creative.

Vocabulary builder

Positive and negative expressions

1 Complete the table below by putting these phrases into categories, according to whether they are positive or negative.

to go unrecognized   to fall at the last hurdle   to meet your objectives
to make a dream come true   to backfire   to come to nothing   to fall on your feet
to achieve your full potential   to go from strength to strength
to not cut the mustard   to bomb   to fulfil an ambition   to go down the drain
to hit the jackpot   to fall by the wayside   to go belly up   to go according to plan
to leave something to be desired

positive	negative

2 Complete these sentences using some of the phrases from Exercise 1 in the correct form. In some cases, more than one answer is possible.

1 Not everyone gets to .... However, the sense of purpose that comes from aiming to do so is, in a way, its own reward.
2 Not every success story makes it into the headlines, and despite what might be implied by newspapers that follow the careers of the celebrities, it is all too often the case that achievements ....
3 We had a new sales manager and he seemed to be destined for the top, but after three weeks, we decided he just couldn't ...., so we had to let him go.
4 I wrote 12 eBooks which sold a few hundred copies each, but I finally .... with my 13th eBook, selling over 400,000 copies.
5 I invested £200,000 in a new software company, but unfortunately the company ...., and I lost the money.

3 Write four more sentences using some of the other phrases in Exercise 1.

4 Look back at the text on pages 93–94 and find at least eight expressions relating to success and/or failure.

Example: highly valued

5 Discuss these questions with a partner.

1 What is the difference between success in sport and business?
2 What are the qualities of a successful student?
3 How do you measure success in life?
4 Is there too much emphasis on trying to be successful, given that only a few people manage to reach the top?

Success and failure

6 Complete these quotes with the correct form of *success* or *failure*. You may need to change the noun to an adjective or verb.

1 If at first you don't ...., try, try again. (*William E. Hickson*)
2 .... is the opportunity to begin again more intelligently. (*Henry Ford*)
3 The only real .... in life is the .... to try. (*anon*)
4 Behind every .... man is a wise woman. (*anon*)
5 When one door closes, another door opens; but we often look so long and so regretfully at the closed door that we .... to see the ones which open for us. (*Helen Keller*)
6 Anyone who says '............................' is not in their vocabulary should buy a better dictionary. (*anon*)
7 A man may .... many times, but he isn't a .... until he begins to blame somebody else. (*Robert Browning*)
8 Haste in every business brings .... (*Herodotus*)
9 A .... person is one who can build firm foundations with the bricks that others throw at him or her. (*Ralph Waldo Emerson*)
10 What we call .... is not the falling down, but the staying down. (*Mary Pickford*)

7 The expressions in 1–7 below contain a number of useful collocations, but each set contains one word/expression that does not form a collocation. First, use your dictionary to find which word/expression does not belong in each set. Then choose the correct collocation to complete each of the sentences, making any necessary changes.

1 **make *a success / your fortune / a deal / a failure***
OK, let's .... I'll let you have the car with air conditioning if you sign the contract today.
2 **hit *rock bottom / back / the success / the jackpot / the nail on the head / the spot***
Shortly after I took over the company, it ...., but in the last three years, we have gradually recovered and we should be in the black next year.
3 **lose *sight of / touch / a fortune / your job / an idea / your life / interest / your balance / your mind***
When the housing bubble burst, I .... and I now have precisely £14.37 in the bank.
4 **gain *practice / access / independence / weight / ground / a reputation***
We aren't the market leaders yet, but we're .... on our biggest competitor.
5 **win *the lottery / new customers / people's respect / a prize / the election / hands down / some decisions / a contract***
When our products are entered into a competition with our competitors, ours .... every time, as they are so much more efficient.
6 **deserve *a holiday / failure / a mention / careful consideration / a medal***
Considering all the work you've done, you really do ....
7 **earn *a living / your car / a fortune / a reputation / your keep***
It takes quite a few years for you to .... as a competent and successful lawyer.

8 Think of sentences in which the other collocations in Exercise 7 could be used.

Spotlight on language

Understanding the author's point of view

1 For each of these sentences, decide whether the author is being positive, negative or neutral. For the positive and negative ones, underline the key words which helped you find the answer. Circle words any that you think were distractors.

1 It's true that when Alex took over the club there were many problems, but under his leadership, it has gone from strength to strength.
2 France has always had an excellent reputation for high-quality food, but many French students these days will grab a burger for lunch, so I think the future of French cuisine is uncertain.
3 Many people hire barges on the various canals in England and spend one or two weeks cruising around with their family.
4 Following the stock-market crash, there was a spectacular decline, and as yet there is no light at the end of the tunnel.
5 The electric car has seen both technical advances and also a number of setbacks, so the jury is still out on its future.
6 While the motor car produces pollution and causes accidents, the benefits it brings in terms of increased mobility and transport of goods far outweigh the negative aspects.
7 Despite a promising start, it looks like the company will soon be facing bankruptcy.
8 The reason many people set up their own business is to make money, despite what they say about fulfilment and personal satisfaction.

Patterns in a text

Poor readers tend to read a text as a sequence of individual words that make up individual sentences, whereas a good reader will look for how ideas are presented through patterns in a text. You first looked at patterns in the text in Unit 5 (pages 59–61). The seven examples in Exercise 2 will take you a little further.

2 Match these text patterns (1–7) with the statements below and on page 97 (a–g).

1 statement + example
2 problem + solution
3 question + answer
4 history + sequence of events
5 description + evaluation
6 for + against
7 compare + contrast

a My father runs a printing business, which was set up in 1899 by his great grandfather. They moved to new premises in 1922 and have continued to expand since then. They were the first company to use colour printing in newspapers and were one of the first to go digital in the 1980s.

b For many years, rim brakes were the only kind available to cyclists, but in recent years, disk brakes have become popular. While both types of brake perform the same function, the disk brakes are more effective in wet weather. Rim brakes are significantly cheaper and are also easier to maintain, so remain popular with some cyclists.

c Making organ donation opt-out rather than opt-in means that many more lives will be saved. However, some people are uncomfortable with the idea of people being pressured into organ donation and feel it should be up to the individual to opt in.

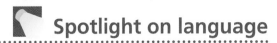

d Just what kind of education is best for business leaders of the future? Undoubtedly one that offers a solid grasp of economics as well as modern languages.
e Large numbers of children in some parts of the world suffer from blindness. The simple addition of vitamin C to their diet could prevent this devastating problem.
f Having studied at the Hopewell Institute for three years, I have to say that I have been very happy. The facilities are top class, the training is second to none, and I am confident that I will get a great job as a result.
g There are some things that America can do more effectively than Europeans. For example, measles has been eradicated from the Americas, but is still common in Europe.

Note that the two parts can often be reversed, but with a slight change of emphasis. For example, in item g above:

Measles has been eradicated from the Americas, but is still common in Europe. There are some things that America can do more effectively than Europeans.

Here, the example in the second sentence now reads as a judgment and forms a stronger conclusion than in the original.

3 Look at the underlined words and phrases in this text and answer the questions below to help you decide what the expressions tell you about the writer's opinions about Clive Sinclair and his invention, the C5.

1985 Sinclair C5

Sir Clive Sinclair was a **1** very rich, **2** eccentric genius who **3** amassed a fortune in the manufacture of **4** revolutionary – indeed **5** visionary – electronic devices and products. These included calculators, watches, meters, pocket TVs (1975), micro-computers (1980) and home computers (1982, when computers were still in dedicated rooms).

Like TVs and computers, the idea of producing an electric vehicle had been **6** a constant preoccupation for him. In the '70s, ecological issues were in the forefront, and the British government passed legislation that allowed electric-assisted cycles to be used without a licence, as long as they didn't exceed 15mph.

The much-publicized launch was **7** an unqualified disaster. It was held in the middle of winter and the C5s skated on the snow. The press was **8** merciless. Safety and Advertising Standards organizations got involved. Sales and production **9** nosedived, and the company **10** was wound up in October of the same year.

adapted from www.microcarmuseum.com

1 Does the author feel that Sir Clive has too much money, or is the author simply stating a fact?
2 Most people would be happy to be called a genius. What effect does the addition of the word *eccentric* have on the statement?
3 Do you feel *amassing a fortune* is positive, negative or neutral?
4 Positive, negative or neutral?
5 Positive, negative or neutral?
6 Positive, negative or neutral?
7 The author could have said *The launch didn't go quite as Sir Clive had wished.* What is the difference between this sentence and the original?
8 Can you think of other words to describe the reaction of the press? Through the use of the word *merciless*, how did you think the author saw the comments from the press?
9 What other words could the author have used instead of *nosedived*?
10 What other words could the author have used instead of *was wound up*?

Spotlight on exam skills 2

What is the author saying?

Questions in the Reading Paper often depend on understanding the intended function of sentences.

1 Match the pairs of sentences below (a–f) with the functional category (1–6) to which they belong.

1 opinions
2 statements of fact
3 generalizations
4 paraphrases of the same information
5 opposites
6 deductions

a
- The number of cancer patients surviving more than ten years has increased by 21% in the last 40 years.
- Certain insects are regarded as pests, which is why people attempt to control them by using insecticides and other techniques.

b
- Tenzing Norgay was a Nepalese mountaineer who partnered Sir Edmund Hilary on the first ascent of Everest.
- Everest was first climbed by two men: Sir Edmund Hilary and his climbing partner, Tenzing Norgay from Nepal.

c
- People who take drugs to enhance their sporting performance should be banned for life.
- Harvard is undoubtedly the best university for someone hoping to go into business.

d
- To be successful in business, it is very important to get along with people and fit in so that people appreciate your company and want to do business with you.
- It may be surprising to hear, but most successful businesspeople describe themselves as not particularly social. They require that distance to make ruthless decisions which may be painful, but will ultimately benefit the company.

e
- As the number of animal experiments has gone down dramatically but the number of new drugs remains constant, it is likely that far fewer products are tested on animals compared to 30 years ago.
- Nineteen British prime ministers all went to the same school – Eton College – so sending your child to Eton could seriously increase the chances of your son or daughter becoming Prime Minister.

f
- Americans tend to be heavier than other nationalities, but on the whole, their dentistry is probably the best in the world.
- People with tattoos are far more likely to go to prison than those without tattoos.

2 Now choose four of the functional categories from Exercise 1 and write a sentence about what you did yesterday for each one.

Yes / No / Not Given

These questions are quite similar to True / False / Not Given (TFNG) questions, the difference being that the TFNG questions ask you to look at information in the text and decided whether the **information** in the question is true, false or not given. In Yes / No / Not Given questions, you are asked to consider the writer's **opinion** about a particular subject, so you may not be focusing on one specific piece of information but a general impression you get from the text.

Tips

1. Read the statement carefully so you know exactly what you are looking for.
2. The statements are always in sequence through the text, so you don't need to go back to the beginning – simply keep reading for the next answer.
3. When you read the text, if you think the statement may or may not be true because specific detail is lacking, then the answer is 'Not Given'.
4. If the statement contradicts the writer's opinion, the answer is 'No'.
5. Watch out for those distractors! A common one is that the statement refers to an opinion but not the writer's opinion. Remember that one way to make a judgment about something is to use a comparative structure, so pay attention to these.

3 Read this text and do the exam tasks that follow on pages 100–103.

READING PASSAGE 1

You should spend about 20 minutes on Questions 1–13, which are based on Reading Passage 1 below.

The case for cycling to school

All parents want the very best for their children, particularly when it comes to schools and school life. Of course, they not only expect the school to take care of the mental needs of their children but also – and this has been subject to great neglect in the last 20 years – their physical needs.

People appreciate that money is tight, and nobody enjoys paying taxes, but there is a growing feeling that something needs to be done about children's health, and many believe that schools and the government have a big responsibility. Twenty-five years ago, many children either cycled or walked to school. Very few children were taken to school by mummy or daddy. The percentage today? Just 1% of primary pupils and 2% of secondary pupils cycle to school. Many parents will say that roads these days are too dangerous, that they HAVE to drive their children to school. The number of children being driven to school has doubled in the last 20 years. So one reason that the roads are dangerous is because so many parents drive their children to school – the infamous 'school run'. Is this a vicious circle out of which we cannot escape? This is a hotly contested topic, and if a solution is to be found, it will take the co-operation of the government, local authorities, schools, parents, and perhaps most importantly, school pupils.

Very few people are suggesting that the government should ban parents from driving their children to school. What many would like to see is a lot more effort put into promoting cycling. The government should build networks of cycle paths radiating out from schools and suitable cycle-parking facilities at school. Organizations like Sustrans, a UK charity supporting sustainable transport by encouraging people to travel on foot, by bike or by public transport, do their best to help schools, but not all schools want to co-operate. This sometimes goes to bizarre extremes. In Portsmouth, a woman wanted her son to cycle to school, but the school really didn't want him to; however, agreement was successfully reached – on the condition that his mother drove behind him and picked up his bike when he reached school and took it home again, reversing the process in the afternoon.

But if the case is to be won, it is not good enough to rely on anecdotal evidence. So what are the relevant facts in this issue? Well, let's take a look at children's health for a start. In 1995, around 10.9% of boys and 12% of girls between the ages of two and 15 were obese. By 2007, those figures had jumped to 16.8% and 16.1% respectively. By 2050, scientists have predicted that 70% of girls and 55% of boys will be obese.

True, diet has an effect on this, but physical exercise not only helps you maintain a healthy body weight, but also leads to healthy bone development, a strong muscle and cardiovascular system and improved co-ordination. Interestingly, a study in California showed a direct link between children's fitness levels and academic scores in literacy and numeracy. Those in the fittest category scored twice as high as those in the lowest fitness category.

Not only can cycling make you fitter and smarter, it also gives you a great sense of independence. You decide when you cycle home, whether you stop on the bridge to look at the fish, whether you go past the bakery with the fantastic smells or whether you just go straight home and read a good book. Children who are driven to and from school don't have these options. They are dependent on an adult – not something many children want.

Providing safe cycle routes and encouraging children to cycle will not only improve their physical and mental well-being and their sense of independence, it will also lead to a reduction in congestion and pollution in the area where they live. Children will not be the only ones to benefit, as the cycle routes would not just be for children. Anyone could use them to travel around, go shopping, visit friends, etc. without needing a car (which could save families thousands of pounds a year).

Sustrans has started developing such cycle routes and they have had great success with the work they've done. For example, in the town of Market Harborough, they added 17 miles of cycle routes. But the big question is, are the residents of Market Harborough actually getting on their bikes? The answer is a resounding 'yes'. There are 400,000 trips a year on the path, 50,000 of these trips made by children – not bad for a town with a population of just 21,000. Interestingly, 38% of the people using the path could have made the same journey by car, but chose not to.

So what of the future? Will we allow the vicious circle to continue so that more and more children are driven to work because of the congested, polluted and dangerous roads? Or will we give our children the opportunity to ride a bike to school along uncongested, unpolluted and, most of all, safe cycle paths? The answer appears blindingly obvious, but whether we as a society have the willpower to carry out the necessary work remains to be seen.

Questions 1–5

Do the following statements agree with the views of the writer in Reading Passage 1?

Write

YES *if the statement agrees with the views of the writer*
NO *if the statement contradicts the views of the writer*
NOT GIVEN *if it is impossible to say what the writer thinks about this*

1 Schools have given insufficient attention to the physical well-being of children.
2 Sustrans could work harder to ensure the co-operation of schools.
3 The case of the mother following her child in her car is not untypical.
4 Cycling can help children develop a degree of responsibility for themselves.
5 Society in general will clearly encourage more children to cycle to school.

Questions 6–9

Complete the sentences below.
*Choose **NO MORE THAN TWO WORDS** from the passage for each answer.*

6 According to the writer, schools are guilty of the .... of certain needs of children in recent times.
7 Twice as many children are .... to school compared to 20 years ago.
8 There has been a massive increase in the number of .... children.
9 Research indicates there is a strong connection between .... and achievement at school.

Questions 10–13

*Complete each sentence with the correct ending, **A–E**, below.*

10 A school in Portsmouth
11 A study in California
12 The population of Market Harborough
13 A team of scientists

A expects to see high levels of overweight children in the future.
B is not keen to see children cycling.
C has suggestions for improving literacy and numeracy.
D supports and develops cycle routes for children.
E enjoys the benefits of new cycle routes.
F does not rely on anecdotal evidence.

READING PASSAGE 2

You should spend about 20 minutes on Questions 14–27, which are based on Reading Passage 2 below.

Questions 14–19

Reading Passage 2 has six sections, **A**–**F**.

Choose the correct heading for each section from the list of headings below.

List of Headings

- **i** Tough words that have to be said
- **ii** Passion leads to great coffee
- **iii** Getting the message out
- **iv** Preparing young people for employment
- **v** Too much emotion
- **vi** A harder time ahead
- **vii** Back to school
- **viii** Results are not enough
- **ix** Preparing for change

14 Section A ....
15 Section B ....
16 Section C ....
17 Section D ....
18 Section E ....
19 Section F ....

Should we recalibrate what we think of as success?

'High Mistress' Clarissa Farr believes that a rounded education and realistic expectations are as important as top exam grades for her pupils at St Paul's.

'There's far too much passion everywhere these days; we're drowning in it,' observes Clarissa Farr, the head of the elite private St Paul's School for Girls in west London, with a note of dry humour.

She is referring, however, not to the age-old problem of broiling teenage hormones, but the modern phenomenon of shamefully over-excitable adults.

A ....

'We were interviewing various companies about designing a new prospectus, and they were all declaring how passionate they were,' she elucidates.

'Cafés put signs up announcing their passion for serving coffee or making sandwiches – and it's a reflection of how overhyped the world has become. Our society has been in thrall to the max; maximum working, maximum earning, maximum reaction, and the extreme language is a symptom of that.

'An important part of my role is to teach intelligent restraint, to turn the temperature down and encourage my girls to take a step back and engage in thought rather than simply adding their voices to the confusion.'

B ....

Of late, Miss Farr has been sharing her intelligent thoughts with us all. She has written to newspapers to give her opinions on the character-building importance of extra-curricular challenges. She has made headlines with the revelation that she was staging parenting classes at her school, which counts Rachel Weisz, the actress; Alexandra Shulman, the editor-in-chief of *Vogue*; Jennifer Saunders, the comedian; Stephanie Flanders, the BBC economics editor; and Carol Thatcher, the journalist among its alumnae – the Old Paulinas.

C ....

Right now, Miss Farr, officially known as the High Mistress, is calmly saying the unsayable; namely that even young people who attend top-flight places of learning such as hers will struggle to find employment. 'We need to prepare young people for the world as it is now, not as we would wish it to be,' she says crisply.

'This generation I'm looking at now isn't going to be chasing super-salaries. A lot are going to struggle to get employment – at present, the best-educated graduates are coming out of university without jobs.'

Cue gasps of anguish from pushy parents everywhere, but Miss Farr, 54, tall and impeccably dressed, cuts an imposing figure who brooks no argument. She commands respect within the school walls and far beyond; when she speaks, educationalists listen. Her school's liberal ethos – embodied in the absence of uniform – is balanced by its mission to 'educate the prodigiously gifted'. Miss Farr is unabashed by this elitist reputation, but believes that a rounded education instils more than a rigorous work ethic.

D ....

Today's teenagers will need more than just a series of top exam grades if they are to shine. Resourcefulness, confidence and a flexible mindset will be just as – perhaps even more – important.

'We need to recalibrate what we think of as success. What will success look like in the future? Most probably not a job for life, and that process of altering perspective begins at school.'

Recalibration doesn't come cheap; after shelling out fees of £18,000 a year, parents could be forgiven for assuming that their daughters will be able to pick and choose their own career paths.

Given the current pressure on leading universities to admit more students from the state sector, Old Paulinas might even find the odds are, for the first time in the school's 108-year history, stacked against them.

But Miss Farr refuses to complain at what is perceived by other independent head teachers as a blatant unfairness.

E ....

'When our girls go to interview for university places, they're given a tough time, and quite rightly so,' she says. 'They've had access to excellent teaching and have had the opportunity to hear extraordinary speakers from a whole range of professions. This is a high-octane intellectual environment, and they should have to work harder to prove themselves.'

Miss Farr, who is married to John Goodbody, the sports journalist, has two children: a 16-year-old daughter and a 14-year-old son, both of whom are at single-sex independent schools.

As a parent, she can empathise with other parents' concerns. 'A school like this can have a reputation for being detached and stand-offish,' she says. 'But we see ourselves as working alongside parents in bringing up their girls. What have been billed in the press as "parenting classes" are more a sort of seminar, a forum where parents can meet and share experiences.'

F ....

Miss Farr has bluntly pointed out to high-flying professional parents who work long hours and often travel abroad that they are 'deceiving themselves if they think they can bring up children by iPhone'. It's not necessarily the message today's hard-pressed parents want to hear, but it is, avers Miss Farr, the message they need to hear.

Subjects under discussion thus far have included the Internet, discipline and, most recently, how to support girls through the stressful exam period. Needless to say, the high-achieving girls of St Paul's won't turn a hair at the plan by Michael Gove, the Education Secretary, to let universities preside over the setting of significantly tougher A-levels.

Some state schools however, will find it a tough readjustment. But Miss Farr – disingenuously, perhaps – claims that there is no gulf between the two sectors. 'I don't see a divide; the independent sector is another component within a mosaic of provision that includes faith schools, academies and the maintained sector,' she says.

'In this school, we have a very particular purpose: to look after the needs of very academically gifted girls. That's our contribution, and through our bursary and outreach work, we are trying to be as accessible as we can to any girls who would benefit.'

But education isn't just about the students; effective learning begins with good teaching, but the pressures of the job mean that as in the state sector, the independent sector is facing something of a leadership crisis.

'There are not enough people wanting to go into the top job; nobody wants to be the one held responsible,' says Miss Farr. 'A generation of deputy heads needs to be encouraged to stand up and become the point beyond which the buck can't be passed.'

Much of the mistrust felt by those in school management stems from the way education is invariably treated as a political football. 'I feel very strongly that education needs to stand outside political motivations; one of the problems we face is that as every new government comes to power, we are forced to swing between policies.

'We need a slow-burn, evolutionary strategy that will serve us for the long haul. At the moment, there's a lot of integrated thinking, which is encouraging, as it fosters a bespoke rather than a one-size-fits-all approach to providing education.' At St Paul's School for Girls, where learning is tailored to the proverbial crème de la crème, Miss Farr is in her element and keen to proselytize to those considering education as a career.

'It's up to schools to rebalance people's thinking and reset the co-ordinates for a different kind of future. Shaping young people's values is an important, exciting role.'

adapted from www.telegraph.co.uk

Questions 20–23

Do the following statements agree with the information given in Reading Passage 2?

Write

TRUE *if the statement agrees with the information*
FALSE *if the statement contradicts the information*
NOT GIVEN *if there is no information on this*

20 Miss Farr's ideas are only relevant for parents and pupils of St Paul's School.
21 Miss Farr has an unwelcome message about the future of her pupils.
22 Miss Farr abandoned school uniform as part of the school's philosophy.
23 Miss Farr believes business success can lead to poor parenting decisions.

Questions 24–27

Choose the correct letter, ***A****,* ***B****,* ***C*** *or* ***D****.*

24 St Paul's School is
A a school with special classes for emotional teenagers.
B one of the best state schools in London.
C facing financial problems which will require it to modify its policies.
D under the direction of a woman with strong views.

25 Miss Farr believes
A companies should demonstrate a passion for work.
B people should reflect before taking action.
C parents need exams in parenting.
D some pupils will not want jobs with high-paying salaries.

26 The writer predicts that the reaction to Miss Farr's views on future employment prospects will be
A heard by educationalists.
B shocking to some parents.
C useful to the young people at St Paul's.
D seen by society as elitist.

27 There is a leadership crisis
A because there are not enough deputy heads in schools.
B as a result of a series of recent political changes.
C in schools in both the independent sector and the state sector.
D in management teams as they lack trust in government.

CLASSROOM WORKOUT

Deciding factors

- In small groups, choose two out of these three things:
  - a sports team
  - a young person starting out on a career
  - a product that has recently come onto the market.
- Discuss in your groups what factors can influence whether the team, person or product will be a success or a failure.
- Present your ideas to the other groups. They will then decide who or what is most likely to ultimately succeed – or fail.

CHECK YOURSELF

- In this unit, you read about some successful people and organizations. Write down some of the qualities that they have.
- Consider how such qualities could be taught in schools.

SUMMARY

In this unit, you:

- looked at phrases and collocations connected with success and failure. Did you learn any new ones?
- studied ways of looking for the author's point of view. When you read a newspaper, is it clear to you whether the piece is fact or opinion?
- worked with patterns in a text. Do you now notice such patterns when you read?
- read a text about the Sinclair C5. Did you check it out online? Would you like to buy one?
- studied **Yes / No / Not Given** questions. Why is it important to check whose opinion is given in the different parts of a text?
- revised **multiple-choice** questions. Which do you find easier, the sentence-completion multiple choice or the question-and-answer multiple choice?
- read a text about St Paul's School. If you had the money, would you send your daughter there?

Over to you

1 Successful people often work exceedingly long hours, and while they have a lot of money in the bank, they don't have time to spend with the friends and family. Go online or find articles about people who:
   - have worked hard for success
   - are rich, but not happy
   - are not inspired by a life of material rewards.

   What patterns do you notice in those texts?

2 You read about Clive Sinclair and his visionary ideas. The IELTS test often contains passages about a creative idea. Do you know any creative people in your country? Find out about innovative and creative people in an article or on the Internet. What encouraged them to be successful?
   How should society encourage such people?

3 Find some short texts where the writer expresses opinions and create some Yes / No / Not Given questions about them. Give them to your colleagues and see if they can answer them.

UNIT 9 Networks

In this unit, you will:
- discuss different sorts of groups and networks
- study and practise **classifying information** tasks
- study and practise **matching features / locating information** tasks.

Getting started

1 What are the advantages and disadvantages of being part of these groups?

1

4

2

5

3

6

2 Which photos do you associate with these expressions?

a sense of belonging   like-minded individuals   depending on one another
sharing the workload   shared values   friendly rivalry   learning discipline
putting the group first   pooling your resources   survival of the fittest
standing out from the crowd   working as a team   enjoying one another's company
knowing one another's strengths and weaknesses

3 Decide whether the extracts below (1–12) refer to groups of:

A people
B animals
C things.

1 After spending some time at the river following a long migration across the plains, the herd moved off into the distance, continuing their journey.
2 When the bells ring, the whole crew springs into action with a minimum of fuss. That is the result of weeks of practice drills in training.
3 The plan misfired when an alert member of the public called the police. The gang managed to escape, although one was soon captured and put behind bars.
4 It's the time of year when they arrive in great numbers: great flocks descend on the lakes each day, and the air is filled with their songs, their warnings and their fighting for territory.
5 There were stacks of them all over the floor, dusty volumes that had been unread for years.
6 There are, of course, a host of reasons why this happened, some of which will be explored in the next section.
7 The jury took the best part of a day to reach a decision.
8 It was nothing but a pack of lies from start to finish, and I can't imagine anyone being foolish enough to believe a single word.
9 Swarms can be dangerous, so you have to treat them with respect. The last thing you want to hear is the buzz of a thousand angry individuals coming your way.
10 In autumn, they fall and lie in great multicoloured heaps on the paths around the estate.
11 It was the highlight of my trip: hearing the roars of the pride and then watching as they came into view.
12 They managed to push through the throng towards the front in the hope of getting a better view. But the problem was that everyone at the festival seemed to have the same idea.

4 Match the extracts in Exercise 3 (1–12) with these words (a–l).

a lions **b** bees **c** criminals **d** books **e** explanations **f** sailors
g birds **h** crowds **i** leaves **j** stories **k** people **l** wildebeest

5 Look back through extracts 1–12 in Exercise 3 and find at least two more useful expressions for each of the categories in this table.

quantity	time
a minimum of fuss	spending some time
movement	**relating to behaviour**
a long migration across (the plains)	springs into action

Spotlight on language 1

Describing groups

We often use the structure '*the* + adjective' to refer to a group:
the rich, the lonely, the fittest

Similar structures are '*those* (*who are/were*) or *anyone* (*who is/was*) + adjective/*–ed* form of the verb':
those interested, those concerned, anyone involved
***Those interested** should come to my office tomorrow.*
***Anyone who is concerned** about the environment will want to read this article.*

Match these expressions to make pairs with more or less opposite meanings.

1 the disabled	**a** the living
2 the wealthy	**b** those unscathed
3 the weak	**c** the able-bodied
4 the old	**d** those unfamiliar (with sth)
5 the innocent	**e** the strong
6 the dead	**f** the young
7 the injured	**g** the average
8 the unwary	**h** those responsible
9 the gifted	**i** the needy
10 the experienced	**j** the cautious

Two further variants of the structure:

1 *The university is especially worried about students who are at risk of failing the course through non-attendance.*
= *The university is especially worried about **those at risk** of failing the course through non-attendance.*

2 *Anyone who hopes / is hoping to leave early after the meeting will have to obtain permission first.*
= ***Anyone hoping** to leave early after the meeting will have to obtain permission first.*

Spotlight on exam skills 1

Classifying

In the exam, you might be asked to classify information in some way. This is in fact a form of matching information from the text.

Examples you could be asked to classify include:

- characteristics and who/what they belong to
- dates or periods and events that happened then
- opinions and people who held them
- places and features associated with them.

Tips

1 Read the question carefully so you know what information to look for.
2 Scan the reading passage to locate the information.
3 Underline the key element you have to classify.
4 Remember that the information could be in several different places.
5 Check to see if the information is in direct speech or is reported in the text.
6 Check whether answers can be repeated.

Read this text and do the task on page 109.

READING PASSAGE 1

You should spend about 20 minutes on Questions 1–13, which are based on Reading Passage 1.

Getting connected

A We tend to think of social networks are being distinctly human. In fact, they occur wherever animals live in 'bonded' groups – where individuals gather together because of their personal relationships rather than being forced to by environmental factors such as a food source or safe sleeping site. Bonded groups are found among all primates and a few other mammals including whales and dolphins, dogs, horses and elephants.

B Group living needn't tax your intelligence too much. In a loose herd, clues such as body size or aggressiveness may be enough to judge whether you should challenge or steer clear of another individual. Those hoping to lead a relatively untroubled life just need to pay attention to the clues. In bonded networks, however, you need to know each member's personal characteristics and those of the friends and relations that might come to their aid. Keeping track of the ever-changing web of social relationships requires considerable mental computing power.

C As a reflection of this, there is a correlation between the size of a species' brain and the typical size of its social groups. In other words, brain size seems to place a limit on the number of relationships an individual can have. This link between group size and brain size is found in all animals that form bonded societies. As group size increases, so too does the number of relationships that need servicing.

D But social effort is not spread evenly. Individuals put most effort into their closest relationships to ensure that these friends will help out when they need them. In traditional societies, everyone in the community is literally part of the same family with direct ties to everyone else, either as biological relatives or in-laws. In post-industrial societies, this is no longer true – we live among strangers, some of whom become friends. As a result, our social circles really consist of two different networks – family and friends – with roughly half drawn from each group. We give priority to family, choosing to include them in our networks above those unrelated to us. Indeed, people coming from large extended families actually have fewer friends.

E Family and friend relationships differ in other important ways. One is that friendships are very prone to decay if untended. Failure to see a friend for six months or so leaves us feeling less emotionally attached to them. Family relationships, by contrast, are incredibly resilient to neglect. As a result, the family half of our network remains constant throughout our lives, whereas the friendship component undergoes considerable change over time. Although the average social network contains around 150 friends, there is considerable individual variation. Some people have fewer than 100 relationships, a few may have 250 or more. There are three main reasons for this: gender, social skills and personality.

Social skills are important in juggling the complex and ever-changing world of social relationships. They seem to depend on theory of mind, or mentalizing – the ability to understand another person's perspective. People's abilities at these skills varies, and it turns out that the number of best friends we have correlates with this. Since women tend to be better at mentalizing than men, it is perhaps no surprise that they often have larger social circles than men.

F Personality plays an important role, too. As might be expected, extroverts have larger social circles than introverts. Despite being more social, however, extroverts are not emotionally closer to members of their network than introverts. It seems we have a limited amount of social capital and can either spread it thickly among a few friends or thinly among many.

And what of online relationships? Despite the opportunities that the digital world offers for increased relationships, it is not without its drawbacks. One is the fact that online conversations take place in a bubble. Because we cannot see the people we are talking to, our imaginations run riot. We attribute to them all the most desirable traits that we would wish to find in the perfect partner or best friend. That makes it very easy for predators to lurk in the system and prey on the unsuspecting. Online romantic scams alone are thought to cost victims more than £1 billion a year globally.

G A second potential problem is the fact that children are spending increasing amounts of time online with their friends rather than meeting them face to face. In real life, we must confront our social problems head on, and in doing so, we learn to negotiate our way out of trouble. But if someone upsets us online, we can simply pull the plug. As online social networking grows in popularity, we risk creating a generation that has limited social skills and smaller social networks. In our increasingly urban and globalized world, social networks are already more fragmented than they were for our ancestors, and this could leave people even more isolated and alienated.

adapted from *New Scientist*

Questions 1–7

Reading Passage 1 has seven sections, **A–G**.

Which section contains the following information?
NB *You may use any letter more than once.*

1 the different effort needed to keep some relationships alive
2 the self-interest that is the basis of close relationships
3 the potential dangers of some types of relationship
4 the different reasons for groups to form
5 the impact on problem-solving of some relationships
6 the relationship between mental development and social networks
7 the awareness of individual differences

Questions 8–12

Classify the following characteristics as belonging to

A online relationships.
B relationships in groups that are not bonded.
C relationships in traditional societies.
D relationships in bonded groups.

8 They depend on family size.
9 They are based on easily observable information.
10 They are not exclusive to humans.
11 They can be unrealistic.
12 They are all with relatives.

Question 13

Choose the correct letter, ***A****,* ***B****,* ***C*** *or* ***D****.*

13 The writer comments that social relationships
A will increase the number of close relationships people can have.
B are likely to change for the worse as a result of technology.
C offer different ways of solving problems.
D will take a longer time to develop into real friendships.

Vocabulary builder

Words in context

1 Choose the correct definition, a) or b), for each of the words and expressions from the text on pages 108–109 in bold below.

1 **personal** **a)** the people who work in a company
b) something relating to you

2 **primates** **a)** your close friends
b) ape-like animals

3 **mammals** **a)** animals that give milk to their young
b) animals which live in burrows and are almost blind

4 **loose** **a)** the opposite of *win*
b) the opposite of *tight*

5 **to steer** **a)** to cry uncontrollably
b) to control the direction of a car

6 **correlation** **a)** someone you are related to
b) a link

7 **to spread** **a)** to thinly cover a surface with something
b) to improve dramatically

8 **in-laws** **a)** people involved in keep order in society
b) the relatives of your wife or husband

9 **extended family** **a)** a family whose members live in different places, perhaps in different countries
b) those members of a family beyond brothers, sisters and parents, including cousins and more distant relatives

10 **prone** **a)** susceptible
b) an uneducated person

11 **perspective** **a)** intended meaning
b) a viewpoint

12 **drawbacks** **a)** technical issues
b) negative points

2 Complete these sentences using words or expressions from Exercise 1.

1 It is good to listen to people of a different generation, as they can bring a different .... to a discussion.
2 I prefer to wear ....-fitting clothes, as I feel a lot more relaxed that way.
3 When time-share agents are trying to sell you a property, they are keen to stress the benefits, but are strangely unwilling to talk about the ....
4 I have to admit I get on better with my .... than with my own family.
5 .... are, biologically speaking, our closest relatives, and we should make a much better effort to preserve their habitats.

3 Write seven sentences using the words/expressions from Exercise 1 that you did not use in Exercise 2.

Spotlight on language 2

Oppositions and contrasts

Texts are often constructed around a series of oppositions and contrasts. Paying attention to such oppositions can help you predict what the text is going to say. In addition, they can help you guess the meaning of new words or expressions.

1 Which of these pairs of opposites are found in Reading Passage 1 (pages 108–109), and in which paragraphs?

1	past time	present time	paragraph G
2	men	women	
3	children	adults	
4	humans	animals	
5	fact	theory	
6	thoughts	feelings	
7	friends	strangers	
8	change	resistance to change	
9	reality	imagination	
10	safety	danger	
11	big	small	

Comparing and contrasting

Texts with oppositions or contrasts will often contain direct or indirect comparisons. These are frequently used in questions to check whether you have understood the meaning and construction of the reading passage.

2 Put these phrases used when comparing and contrasting into the correct column of the table below.

similar identical akin unlike in contrast alike likewise
have a lot in common (bear) a resemblance tell the difference
distinguish between tell apart look the same by contrast
differ in many respects similarly a striking similarity
there's no comparison huge contrast discrepancy between unique
in the same vein share an opinion follow someone's lead

concentrating on difference	concentrating on similarity

3 Complete each of these sentences with a suitable phrase from the table in Exercise 2.

1 There are many sub-species of tuna fish; they might look .... to you and me, but an expert can .... them.
2 I once met a woman who said there was .... between me and Johnny Depp, though I can't see it myself.
3 Societies in which there is a big .... between the incomes of rich and poor people tend to have a lot of crime.
4 In Sweden, taxes are high, but the state looks after all its citizens when they need help, ... in some countries where taxes are comparatively low but there is little help for people who desperately need it.
5 My brother and I don't .... He drives a sports car and lives a jet-setting lifestyle. I don't have a car and grow most of my own vegetables.
6 The brain, ... computers, does not have to follow logical patterns and is capable of great innovation.
7 Everyone is .... , even twins who look .... and whom most people could not ....
8 It was an oral exam, but it felt more .... to a friendly conversation to the student, who wondered if the examiner felt ....
9 The first day was spent on safari counting the number of wild animals drinking at watering holes. Days 2 and 3 pretty much passed .... as the researchers tried to assess the health of the animals in the area.
10 Penguins gather at the edge of the ice, not wanting to be the first to dive in, in case there should be a polar bear waiting beneath the ice. But once one brave soul has dived, the others very soon .... and plunge into the water.

4 Complete these sentences so they are true for you.

1 My country has a lot in common with ...
2 The way I was educated differs in many respects from ...
3 The problems my generation faces today are unlike ...
4 In my opinion, there's a huge contrast between ...
5 Unlike when I was growing up, ...

5 In the next section, you are going to read a text about multi-tasking. What, if anything, do you think it will say about these contrasts?

1 saving time / wasting time
2 physical tasks / mental tasks
3 myth / reality
4 brain / computer
5 receiving information / processing information
6 simple activities / complex activities
7 men / women
8 young / old
9 at work / at home
10 nowadays / in the future

Spotlight on exam skills 2

Exam practice

1 Read this passage and do the task on pages 114–115.

READING PASSAGE 2

You should spend about 20 minutes on Questions 14–26, which are based on Reading Passage 2 below.

What is multi-tasking?

Multi-tasking might feel productive, but it can be more dangerous than drink driving and even make you drop IQ points. Multi-tasking is the appearance of being able to handle more than one task at the same time. For decades, humans have grappled with the notion that despite the 100 million neurons in their brains, we actually remain unable to do two things at once. When we talk about multi-tasking, we're really referring to rapidly switching between tasks.

A hot topic of psychological research around the world, particularly in the US, the study of multi-tasking is still in its infancy. Many questions remain unanswered and will only be resolved with time. However, research is showing that the way the human brain functions does not allow multi-tasking to deliver longed-for efficiencies.

Is it a myth?

Many scientists believe the ability to multi-task is a myth. In fact, one psychiatrist has gone so far as to describe it as a 'mythical activity in which people believe they can perform two or more tasks simultaneously as effectively as one'. Unlike computers, which can perform tasks at lightning speed, the human brain needs to switch between tasks, depending on which area of the brain is being used. Multi-tasking often involves goal switching and re-evaluating, which experts say takes time. What appears to be human multi-tasking is more akin to channel surfing between television stations.

Ernst Poppel, of the Institute for Medical Psychology at Munich's Ludwig Maximilian University, believes humans cannot perform two or three tasks at once with the same degree of concentration. He says seemingly simultaneous awareness and information processing takes place in three-second windows. The human brain takes in the data about the environment streaming in from the sensory systems; subsequent events are then processed in the next window. For example, humans can concentrate on a conversation for three seconds, then move their focus to a computer screen for three seconds, and then to a crying child three seconds later. While one task is in the foreground of human consciousness, the others remain in the background until it is their turn to be given access to the central processor in the human brain.

How did the notion of multi-tasking start?

The concept came to the fore with the advent of computers, which have central processing units and can proceed rapidly from one task to another. The notion of multi-tasking appeals because it suggests that more can be achieved within a certain amount of time. It is of particular appeal to employers keen to gain efficiencies. However, research shows usually there is little to be gained by humans switching between tasks.

Does multi-tasking save time?

Research has shown, generally, it doesn't. In fact, it can have the opposite effect. It can take longer to do multiple tasks concurrently than if the focus were on completing one task at a time. Dr Julia Irwin, of Macquarie University's Department of Psychology in Sydney, says the problem with multi-tasking is that the amount of attentional capacity humans have is restricted, and it has to be shared among the several tasks being performed.

When flipping between tasks, humans must pause between switching from one part of the brain to another. This is known as a post-refractory pause and uses precious time. Switching back to the original task takes up more time again.

Research shows it is less time-efficient to switch between tasks, as humans must, than to focus on one task at a time.

Multi-taskers can also be left with a reduced ability to perform each task. Research done in 2004 by Marcel Just, Professor of Psychology at Carnegie Mellon University, asked people to listen to a sentence and then say whether it was true or false at the same time as they rotated an object in their hand. It was found that while people were able to perform both tasks at the same time, it took them twice as long as it did if they focused on each task individually, one after the other.

Professor David E. Meyer, a psychology professor at the University of Michigan, has shown how time is lost when humans shuttle between tasks. People were asked to write a report and check their email at the same time. Those who constantly jumped between the tasks took about one and a half times as long to complete the task as those who completed one job before turning to another.

Given our human limitations, can we actually improve our performance at multi-tasking?

You can improve your multi-tasking ability, but only up to a point. For a long time, people have known that training to perform a particular sequence of tasks can reduce the time it takes if those tasks can become routine. This is because rote tasks require fewer mental demands.

'Those tasks that benefit from practice and which we tend to do well when multi-tasking tend to be ones that can be automated with practice and don't require much attention. So, for example, you can run through in your head what you have to do in the coming day while having a shower,' says Dr Julia Irwin.

However, just because a person has improved their efficiency performing one set of tasks does not mean they have improved their multi-tasking efficiency generally. Research has shown the time lost when switching between tasks increases with the complexity and unfamiliarity of the tasks.

adapted from www.multitaskingtest.net.au

Questions 14–17

Look at the following statements and the list of people below.

*Match each statement with the correct person, **A–D**.*

14 Switching from task to task results in slower performance.
15 Although possible, multi-tasking is time consuming.
16 Multi-tasking works best with undemanding activities.
17 Multi-tasking is in fact the brain focusing on different things for short sequences.

List of People
A Julia Irwin
B Ernst Poppel
C Marcel Just
D David E. Meyer

Questions 18–20

*Choose **THREE** letters, **A–F**.*

*Which **THREE** of these comments about multi-tasking are mentioned by the writer of the text?*

A It is a relatively new area of research.
B Tasks of different degrees of difficulty have been investigated.
C It is only possible with increased levels of attention.
D We can learn from how computers perform tasks.
E It can lead to improved results at work.
F It can have serious consequences.

Questions 21–26

*Complete the summary using the list of words, **A–L**, below.*
***NB** You may use any word more than once.*

Research on multi-tasking

Research into multi-tasking has largely proved that it doesn't work and certainly fails to lead to the **21** .... that had been hoped. Comparisons with computers are inaccurate, as unlike a computer, research shows that the brain appears unable to do two things **22** .... In reality, the work of Ernst Poppel suggests the brain processes input derived from the senses in short **23** .... during which time only one source is in the **24** .... Time is lost, as different tasks involve **25** .... between different areas of the brain and back again. Better results come from focusing on one activity at a time. However, routine tasks that are less **26** .... in terms of attention may be automated, but research indicates that the more challenging the tasks we are engaged in, the longer it takes to do them.

A increases	**G** individually
B pauses	**H** sequences
C switching	**I** efficiencies
D processing	**J** windows
E demanding	**K** attention
F foreground	**L** simultaneously

Tip
If you are unsure of an answer, it helps to classify the different possible answers according to grammar. How many are plural nouns, past tense verbs, adverbs, etc.? Then look at the gap and decide what the grammar category of the missing word is.

2 **Re-read the text and underline all the expressions of opposition or contrast you can find.**

3 a **Find one or more texts that compare different versions of the same thing, for example book or film reviews, product comparisons (e.g. performance tests on three of the latest computers), commentaries on sporting events, historical analysis of past and present, etc.**

b **Make a list of all the features the different things have in common and what is unique to them, and use this to make a classifying activity for a colleague.**

4 a **Make a list of 10–15 expressions of contrast or opposition.**

Example: *unlike, whereas ...*

b **Have a discussion with a partner about the two of you, your experiences and opinions, your background and ambitions, and continue until you have used all the expressions you listed.**

'This project calls for real concentration. Are you still able to monotask?'

www.CartoonStock.com

CLASSROOM WORKOUT

Fitting in or standing out?

- There are pressures on us to conform and be like everyone else, but there are also reasons why it may be good to stand out from the crowd. In small groups, make a list of the advantages and disadvantages of fitting in or standing out.
- Present your ideas to the other groups. Are there any arguments that convince you one way or the other?

CHECK YOURSELF

- In this unit, you read a lot about classification. Taxonomy is the classification of biological organisms; many other things can also be classified, and in a variety of different ways. Look back at the unit to see the kind of classifying you may be asked to look at in the exam, then consider how you might classify at least two of the following:
  - your friends
  - your education
  - places you have visited
  - hotels you have stayed in
  - food in your country.

SUMMARY

In this unit, you:

- looked at expressions about groups of people, animals and things. How many did you write in your notebook?
- read about 'bonded groups'. What can you remember about the characteristics of such societies?
- studied the way texts can be constructed using opposites and contrasts. How common is this feature of texts in this unit?
- practised **classifying** tasks. Why is it important to read the whole text before choosing an answer in this task type?
- read about multi-tasking. How often do you try to do several things at once?

Over to you

1. Read between three and five articles in a newspaper, in a magazine or online. Which forms of oppositions are most common?
2. Find and analyze websites that give advice about maximizing the good use of your time. What advice do they give?
3. Find and read newspaper or online articles about the keys to effective group work. Which ideas do you agree with most?
4. Read versions of the same news story in two different sources. Make a list of what is unique to each version.

UNIT 10 Sport, leisure and time

In this unit, you will:

- discuss different sporting activities
- review and practise different task types
- study and practise some key grammar structures.

Getting started

a

c

e

b

d

1 Look at the five photos. Which activity do you consider the most enjoyable? Which do you consider the least enjoyable? Explain your reasoning.

2 Talk about other sports using these comparative structures.

1 .... is much more fun than ....
2 .... is not as physically challenging as ....
3 .... requires a much higher degree of co-ordination and balance than ....
4 With sports such as .... , the taller you are, the better.
5 While .... is certainly safer than physical sports, some people consider it more of a hobby than a sport, as it only taxes the mind.
6 .... and .... are both activities that involve .... , but in my opinion, ... is the more interesting of the two.
7 All sports require .... , and no less important in many cases is ....
8 Many parents would admit that they are not fans of contact sports, the least popular of which is probably ....
9 You don't need a big investment in equipment if you play .... , which is not the case with ....
10 I think .... is pretty boring as a sport, but .... is even worse.

3 Choose the preposition in italics which best completes these expressions. Are there any expressions which do *not* go with any of the photos on page 117 (a–e)?

1 keep *in / on* shape
2 sense *of / in* adventure
3 work *at / off* steam
4 good *for / in* you
5 build *up / in* an appetite
6 sense *of / for* achievement
7 *in / at* the fresh air
8 have a good work-*out / -on*
9 play *at / in* a team
10 enjoyed *for / by* millions
11 suitable *by / for* all ages
12 risk *of / for* injury
13 compete *over / against*
14 depends *for / on* good hand–eye co-ordination
15 race *for / against* the clock

4 Match the extracts below (1–12) with the activities they describe (a–e).

a mountain biking
b juggling
c golf
d soccer
e none of these

1 This is certainly great for building up your strength, particularly in your leg muscles, which are pumping pretty much all the time.
2 Playing with other people is certainly a pleasure, and the sport needn't be expensive. You can pick up some clubs second hand and play on local courses.
3 Nothing is quite as good for improving hand–eye co-ordination. You have to be aware of speed, trajectory, timing and balance at all times.
4 Outdoor sports have the added attraction of taking place in the fresh air. This sport offers the considerable bonus of helping you enjoy some magnificent scenery as you're speeding along.
5 The thrill of the descent at speed is something you cannot explain if you have not experienced it personally. The world rushes past, but time seems to stand still as you shoot over the snow and ice at incredible speeds.
6 The great thing about this activity is that the sky's the limit. While you can start with three balls, it won't be long before you're doing four or maybe five.
7 This sport is just 22 people chasing after a leather ball. Why on earth is it so popular?
8 Although often considered a sport suitable for the elderly, it is in fact a very fast game that demands a high level of hand–eye co-ordination. The ball travels very fast, and although players don't run great distances, they need to be very agile as they stop and start in short bursts to return the ball as it spins over the net and hits the table.
9 Some people don't class it as a real sport, but you need good upper-body strength and you walk a long way each time you play.
10 This is one sport which seems to unify people from all over the world. Fast action, team tactics and superb skills make this one of the world's most popular sports.
11 The excitement of the downhill rush as you speed down a track through a forest is second to none, and is the reward for the lung-busting struggle uphill.
12 Unlike in some other sports, in this one you don't want to take a lot of shots. In fact, keep out of trouble, and you could be the best.

Spotlight on exam skills 1

Labelling a diagram

In this question type, you will be given a diagram. Examples could include:
- something technical such as a piece of machinery or a new invention
- something from the natural world, e.g. parts of a plant or some aspect of geology
- a design plan for a building (as in the example below).

You will NOT be expected to know about the thing to be labelled; you simply need to understand how the given text relates to the diagram and use words, not always in text order, to label it.

You should:
- have a quick look at the diagram to see what kind of labels are required
- note how many words you can use for the labels
- make sure your words come directly from the text
- check your spelling of the words used in the exercise.

1 Read the text below and label the diagram with no more than THREE words from the text.

New sports club design

As you enter the building through the door on the left, there are two rooms on either side of you: women's changing rooms on the right and men's changing rooms on the left. In the corner of the changing rooms, there are showers. Walking further along the corridor, you can see our equipment room, which we use to store all the balls, nets, mats, etc. Across the corridor from that room is the weight-lifting room, as many sportsmen and women want to work on their strength these days. The two rooms at the end of the corridor are very important ones. On the right is a crèche. Many people who want to visit the sports club don't want to leave their children at home, so the crèche is a play area for young children while their parents are practising sports. Opposite the crèche is our first-aid room. It's reassuring to know that, despite space being at a premium, it's got all the latest equipment for dealing with both slight and serious injuries. The first-aid medic is on hand all the time the centre is open. Both the crèche and the first-aid centre look out onto the main sports hall, which can accommodate tennis, basketball, badminton and five-a-side soccer – though obviously not all at the same time.

As you leave the building, have a look at the fruit trees planted on either side of the entrance to remind people of a healthy lifestyle – three plum trees on your right and three apple trees on your left.

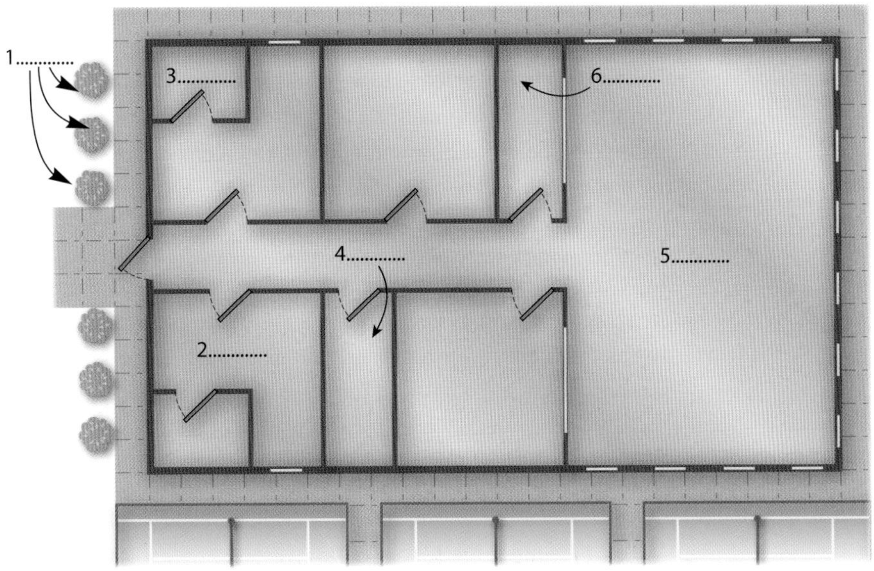

Question-type review

> You have now looked at a whole range of questions that you can expect in the Reading Paper, so there shouldn't be any surprises in the exam itself.
> The following pages review several question types. If you need to jog your memory, look back at the relevant unit.

Unit 1: Multiple-choice questions

2 Which answer(s) do you agree with?

When answering a multiple-choice question, I should:

A read through the whole text carefully to find the answer.

B not put an answer if I don't know it.

C try to eliminate one or two of the options so I can focus on fewer options.

D put two answers down if I feel both could be considered correct.

Unit 1: Paragraph-heading questions

3 Read the paragraphs below (1–3) and choose the most suitable heading (i–vi) for each one. There are three headings you will not need.

List of Headings

i A top tip to save you time

ii Paragraph-heading questions are pretty tough

iii How distractors work

iv Finding the right focus

v Checking answers is crucial

vi Frequent readers see the big picture more easily

1 ....

Quite a few students feel rather daunted by paragraph-heading questions as they rely less on identifying one or two key words but more on a global understanding of the text. Students who are regular readers in English tend to do better on these questions as they find it easier to retain a larger body of text in their head and can make a better decision regarding a suitable paragraph heading.

2 ....

Imagine, for example, there is a text about sport and money; it is very likely that there will be a paragraph heading about sport and another about money, and it is up to you to decide whether the focus of the paragraph is on sport or on money. This is not an easy task, as a lot of thought goes into creating plausible distractors that may appear to be correct, so you have to make sure you understand both the question and the key elements of the paragraph containing the answer.

3 ....

A useful technique that some students forget to use is to cross out each paragraph heading as you find the appropriate paragraph. Using this technique means there are fewer headings to look at each time, saving you valuable seconds which could be used for checking your answers at the end of the exam.

Unit 2: Sentence-completion questions

These are three of the common errors which students make when working with sentence-completion questions.

- They make spelling mistakes when copying the words from the text. If your spelling is not great, make sure you copy the words correctly and check the spelling.
- They write more than the number of words allowed, for which they will be penalized. The most common maximum is three, but always check the rubric.
- Some students, particularly those who are not familiar with the format of the test, will use words that are not found in the text to fill the gaps. This is not allowed.

4 Complete these sentences with no more than TWO words from the box above.

1 One reason some students are penalized is for .... such as *busines* or *examinasion*.

2 The .... number of words allowed is usually three.

3 A clear understanding of the IELTS .... will help you move quickly through the test, as you know what has to be done.

Unit 3: Short-answer questions

Although at first sight short-answer questions seem pretty straightforward, it is surprising how many people trip up on them, not because they don't understand the question and not because they were unable to find the answer, but because they failed to read the rubric properly. If it says NO MORE THAN THREE WORDS, then your answer should not contain more, even if you feel this is a more complete answer. Similarly, the words used must be words FROM THE PASSAGE, even if you feel you could express the answer more effectively with other words.

5 Answer these questions with no more than THREE words from the text above for each answer.

1 What do you have to do carefully so that you know exactly what to do with each question?

2 Where should the words used in the answer come from?

6 Use the text *New sports club design* on page 119 to write questions for which these are the answers.

1 The showers

2 Young children

3 The weight-lifting room

4 The first-aid medic

7 a Go online and find some texts with diagrams that interest you.

b Create IELTS-style questions of the various kinds listed below.

Unit 4: Matching name; Matching sentence ending

Unit 5: Note completion; Summary completion

Unit 6: Chart/Flowchart completion

Unit 7: True / False / Not Given

Unit 8: Yes / No / Not Given

Unit 9: Classifying information

Unit 10: Labelling a diagram

Tip
By creating your own questions, you will gain a better understanding of how the question types work.
If you are working with other people, share your questions with them so that you can all benefit from the experience. Do the questions work? Can you spot the distractors? Can you work out the answers?

8 Work with a partner. How many different types of exam question can you create for this text?

How the battle for Britain's technological future can be won on the playing fields of Eton (and every other school)

These days, it seems all anyone can talk about is how important it is for young people to learn programming skills: a new report has called for making computer science a part of the national curriculum. It's all part of a broader realization that programming and the Science, Technology, Engineering and Maths (STEM) subjects are crucial to our country's success. But what's new? Pretty much every politician agrees that having more young people excel in these subjects would be a good thing, so the important question is how to accomplish it, beyond wishing it to be so.

Part of the problem is incentives. Why should young people put in the hard yards to study these subjects if, on the one hand, you can become a millionaire by working in finance or, on the other hand, you believe that it'd be easier to become (or marry) a footballer or celebrity?

Other issues include teacher quality and the resources available to schools, but one factor that's often overlooked is the unconscious, dismissive attitude that young people, parents and schools have towards programming and STEM subjects. Here's a telling example from an article in the *New Yorker* talking about an American football coach joining a high school in New Jersey and creating an elite team. When he'd arrived at Hackensack High School in 1990, he was surprised to discover that the football players were not the social leaders. 'As time went on, they became the leaders of the school, and the school ran a lot smoother,' he said. 'Younger kids had role models. They said, "I want to be like that guy." If those kids are running the school, you've got a chance.'

It was a stark reminder that athletes – not academics – are considered to be the best role models in schools, not just in the US but also in the UK, where rugby players, football players and other sports stars are held in the highest esteem. And while I have genuine respect for the discipline and work ethic that top student athletes have, none of these virtues are exclusive to sports – and surely, if we're concerned about academic performance, we should be looking at other pursuits that are just as worthwhile and important to students, if not more, than being a fantastic football or rugby player – like programming and STEM.

But instead of starting a fight between sports and STEM, perhaps we should seek to understand why we think that top football players should be natural role models. Here are a few suggestions:

Firstly, sports are competitive, almost to a fault. Competition is highly motivating, particularly in leagues and tournaments – it identifies and rewards successful individuals and teams rather than giving all participants a gold star and a pat on the back. At the same time, sports like cricket, football, and basketball are all about teamwork and co-operation, about forming strong bonds of loyalty and trust; contrast this with the stereotype of scientists as loners, encouraged somewhat by the practice of science in schools.

It can also be seen that sports have clear, understandable and identifiable 'win conditions' – getting the most points or goals. Even if you have two highly skilled teams in a match, anyone watching can understand clearly who's won – in stark contrast to many competitions (in STEM or otherwise) which are decided by the whims of judges conferring in private.

More support for the case for sporting role models comes from the fact that sports are accessible. Anyone can play football, even if they do so badly. This is a hard one for most STEM subjects to emulate, but we're now seeing tools being developed that teach even the youngest children how to program, along with Lego robotics kits for kids. It should not be forgotten that good sports teams have good coaches, whether they're paid employees at schools or volunteers from local teams. We need more academics, engineers and professionals getting stuck in to help schools.

While we might hope that students would study science for purely the love of it, it wouldn't hurt if there was a bit of glory as well. We can't expect STEM subjects or programming to rival sports' attention on national or global stages any time soon, but we can give top science competitions and teams the opportunity to shine in impressive settings. Let's not forget that the 1948 Olympics in London also saw competitions in architecture and literature.

Of course, many schools already hold science fairs and competitions, although, as some teachers have told me, these can often end up looking like either 'who can build the tallest tower out of straws' activities that are entertaining enough for a short while but hardly constitute a genuine challenge, or impressive but hard-to-assess individual experiments. It all feels a bit … easy.

In comparison, we don't blink an eye at kids who play grown-up, full-contact sports for over a dozen hours a week, in rain and shine. We should expect and demand just as much of them in other subjects. Many teenagers have the capacity to program sophisticated games, or design and engineer robots and balloons that go to the edge of space – if they are pushed hard enough and given the right kind of backing and if they are sufficiently motivated through competition and glory.

There are already a few initiatives along these lines, including the excellent US-based FIRST Robotics Competition which sees thousands of teams from high schools across the world building robots to compete in physical games.

Some will argue that turning science and programming into a competition is against the spirit of pure or theoretical science. But we need to remember that science is also about solving concrete problems against impossible odds, whether that's building a bouncing bomb or rescuing astronauts headed to the Moon. Boffins in laboratories or geeks on computers can be just as heroic and inspiring as the best.

If we want our students to excel in programming and STEM, we need to take those pursuits seriously – as seriously as we take sports at school, where parents spend their own money to buy kit and volunteer to drive for hours across the country, where schools build tracks and fields, and where students train after school in the evenings and every weekend. That's how we can make stars.

adapted from www.telegraph.co.uk

Vocabulary builder

Working with context

Scan the text on pages 122–123 to find these ten expressions. Then, without using your dictionary, try to work out what they mean.

to a fault	it wouldn't hurt
a pat on the back	we don't blink an eye
the whims of judges	the right kind of backing
getting stuck in	along these lines
purely for the love of it	against impossible odds

Spotlight on language

Chronology

One of the most important skills in understanding any text is to know what happened when. While texts describing processes often follow a logical chronological sequence of events, many others don't. One reason for this is that a writer may try to grab the reader's attention by starting an account with the most dramatic event, and that could well be something that actually happened towards the end of the story. Another reason is that writers and readers enjoy variety – any text that is wholly predictable would be boring to write and readers would probably not bother to finish it.

1 In each of these sentences, say which of the two underlined expressions happened first.

1 They got married six years after they first met.
2 After they had graduated, they decided to spend six months travelling around the world.
3 Not until we got home did I realize I'd forgotten my laptop.
4 They received their qualification on completing the course.
5 Once you have lived abroad you can really understand cultural differences.
6 The match ended with a victory celebration, but only after the manager had spoken to the players.
7 The discovery of distant planets was made possible by the invention of the telescope.
8 The analysis would not have been possible without the help of modern computers.
9 She had a successful career as a writer and went on to become a government minister.
10 The bulbs bloomed late following a colder-than-expected winter.
11 They won the competition despite previous setbacks.
12 Prior to accepting any position, it is logical to examine the contract.
13 The results would have been published earlier, had it not been for a technical problem.
14 Trials of the new drug began in the winter and subsequently met with official approval.

Time is a crucial factor not only in the IELTS test but also in life itself. The richest person and the poorest person in the world both have exactly 24 hours in a day. Our perception of time can also vary in different situations: the one hour you have for the IELTS Reading Paper will pass very quickly; the time you spend waiting for the result may feel like an eternity!

Paraphrase practice

> It is a primary rule of good writing that the writer should try to interest the reader. One way of doing this is to surprise the reader with new information or unexpected details in each sentence. Repetition is something readers don't normally enjoy, whether it is repetition of ideas, of grammar structures or of expressions – and that's another reason why paraphrasing is such an important skill.

2 For each sentence, choose the word or expression below (a or b) which is closest in meaning to the underlined expression.

1 The smooth running of the project depends on everyone arriving on time.
a) early b) punctually

2 I first became interested in sport when I was 18. I was at university at the time.
a) for a while b) then

3 He worked for some time as a personal coach.
a) This lasted a long time. b) This lasted a short time.

4 You can leave your things here for the time being.
a) temporarily b) as long as you like

5 In my time, students used to spend hours in the library. Now it's all on the Internet.
a) if I remember b) when I was younger

6 By the time she was 21, she was already a champion.
a) before then b) until then

7 I was lucky because I arrived just in time.
a) early b) at the last minute

8 There is only one law of success – be in the right place at the right time.
a) when it is important b) when someone tells you

9 It's about time the system changed.
a) This could happen any time. b) This should have happened before.

10 The new machines can process 1,200 people at a time.
a) simultaneously b) consecutively

11 It's a battle against time.
a) It is important to hurry. b) It is important to finish now.

12 I like to finish ahead of time.
a) as soon as possible b) early

13 You need to have your ID card with you at all times.
a) generally b) always

14 The food here is not brilliant at the best of times.
a) even on a good day b) unless you are lucky

15 This is the best team of all time.
a) ever b) as far as I know

3 Work with a partner. In five minutes, how many different paraphrases can you think of for these sentences?

1 If you want to make progress in anything you do, you have to practise.
2 According to many, technology holds the key to our survival.
3 Everybody likes music, yet most people would find it difficult to say precisely why.
4 Relationships are more important for a happy life than money.

Spotlight on exam skills 2

Exam practice

READING PASSAGE 1

You should spend about 20 minutes on Questions 1–13, which are based on Reading Passage 1.

How we experience time

A The mind does funny things to our experience of time. Just ask French cave expert Michel Siffre. In 1962, Siffre went to live in a cave that was completely isolated from mechanical clocks and natural light. He soon began to experience a huge change in his perception of time. When he tried to measure out two minutes by counting up to 120 at one-second intervals, it took him five minutes. After emerging from the cave, he guessed the trip had lasted 34 days. He'd actually been down there for 59 days. His experience of time was rapidly changing. From an outside perspective, he was slowing down, but the psychological experience for Siffre was that time was speeding up. But you don't have to hide out in a cave for a couple of months to warp time, it happens to us all the time. Our experience of time is flexible; it depends on attention, motivation, the emotions and more.

B People often report that time seems to slow down in life-threatening situations, like skydiving. But are we really processing more information in these seconds when time seems to stretch? Is it like slow-motion cameras in sports which can actually see more details of the high-speed action? In a 2007 test, people stared at a special chronometer while free-falling 50 metres into a net. The results showed that time resolution doesn't increase: we're not able to distinguish shorter periods of time in these conditions. What happens is we remember the time as longer because we record more of the experience. Life-threatening experiences make us really pay attention, but we don't gain superhuman powers of perception.

C We've all experienced the fact that time seems to fly when we're having fun. Or does it? What about when you're listening to a fantastic uplifting piece of music? Does time seem to fly by, or conversely, does it seem to slow down? Tests found that when listeners appreciated the music more, time seemed to slow down. This may be because when we find music pleasant, we listen more carefully, getting lost in it. Paying closer attention leads to perception of a longer interval of time.

D The emotions we feel in the moment directly affect our perception of time. At the end of an exciting day out, it can feel like you ate breakfast a lifetime ago. You had a great time and yet time has stretched out. The fact that we intuitively believe time flies when we're having fun may have more to do with how time seems to slow when we're not having fun. Boredom and negative emotions draw our attention to the passage of time, which gives us the feeling that it's slowing down. Research on anxious cancer patients, those with depression and boredom-prone individuals suggests time stretches out for them.

E Or – prepare yourself for a 180-degree about-face – it could all be the other way around. Perhaps you're having fun when time flies. In other words, we assume we've been enjoying ourselves when we notice that time has passed quickly. There's evidence for this in a recent experiment in which participants doing a boring task were tricked into thinking it had lasted half as long as it really had. They thought it was more enjoyable than those who had been doing exactly the same task but who hadn't been tricked about how much time had passed.

F When things happen very close together in time, our brains fuse them together into a single snapshot of the present. For vision, the shortest interval we can perceive is about 80 milliseconds. If two things happen closer together than that, then we experience them as simultaneous. When we're tired, though, our perception of time becomes extremely unreliable and we find it more difficult to distinguish between short spaces of time. This fact can be used to measure whether people are too tired to fly a plane, drive a truck or be a doctor.

G People often say the years pass more quickly as they get older. While youthful summers seemed to stretch on into infinity, the summers of your later years zip by in the blink of an eye. A common explanation for this is that everything is new when we are young, so we pay more attention; consequently it feels like time expands. With age, though, new experiences diminish and it tends to be more of the same, so time seems to pass more quickly. Whether or not this is true, there is some psychological evidence that time passes quicker for older people. One study has found that people in their 20s are pretty good at guessing an interval of three minutes, but people in their 60s systematically overestimate it, suggesting time is passing about 20% more quickly for them.

H Our experience of time is also affected by who we are. People seem to operate to different beats; we've all met people who work at a much slower or faster pace than we do. Psychologists have found that people who are impulsive and oriented towards the present tend to find that time moves faster for them than others. There's little research on this, but it's likely that each of us has our own personal tempo. Research has found that when different people listen to metronomes, the number of beats per minute (bpm) they describe as comfortable ranges from as slow as 40 bpm up to a high of 200 bpm. This is a large range and may help to explain why some people seem to operate at such a different pace to ourselves.

adapted from www.spring.org.uk

Questions 1–6

Reading Passage 1 has eight paragraphs, **A**–**H**.

Which paragraph contains the following information?
You may use any letter more than once.

1 The role played by individual differences
2 An experiment that manipulated feelings
3 Our perception of time appears enhanced by danger.
4 Lack of light can affect perception of time.
5 Greater appreciation can result in losing track of time.
6 Reactions to negative situations influence time.

Questions 7–12

*Complete each sentence with the correct ending, **A**–**J**, below.*

7 Older people's judgments of the passage of time
8 Psychologists' experiments on people
9 The judgments of the passage of time made by people in their twenties
10 Events that occur very close together in time
11 Devices that measure feelings of tiredness
12 Summers when we were young

A show how wrong our perception of time can be.
B appear to be viewed by the brain as one.
C explain why certain memories seem to diminish.
D indicate that there is a huge variety in our preferred rhythms.
E help people control their impulsive nature.
F seem long because so much was new to us then.
G seem to show that they find less that fixes their attention.
H can prevent people exposing themselves to danger.
I tend to be quite accurate.
J limit what we remember from the past.

Question 13

*Choose the correct letter, **A**, **B**, **C** or **D**.*
Which of the following phrases best describes the main aim of Reading Passage 1?

A to evaluate different experiments on our perception of time
B to examine how time changes the way we feel about events
C to indicate the factors that can influence our perception of time
D to suggest how we can make more effective use of time

CLASSROOM WORKOUT

Debating skills: producing a logical and convincing argument

- In small groups, make plans for a small sports centre that can offer five different sports which should appeal to a wide variety of people.
- Use some of the language you have picked up in the unit to justify your choice of sports.
- Present your ideas to the other groups and listen to their ideas. Can the whole group come to a unanimous choice of five sports?

CHECK YOURSELF

- Look back at the various question types you can expect in the exam. Use the language that you have looked at in this unit to express how you feel about each question type, for example: *I find paragraph-heading questions much harder than multiple-choice questions as they require a more global approach to reading.*

SUMMARY

In this unit, you:

- looked at sports and sporting collocations. Did you pick up many new ones?
- looked at comparative structures. How many can you remember?
- studied expressions with prepositions. Which eight expressions seem most useful to you?
- studied and practised **labelling a diagram**. What are the key points to remember?
- practised a variety of question types. Which ones do you find easy? Which are more difficult?
- practised writing your own IELTS questions. Was it difficult for you?
- looked at some exercises about time. Did you pick up many useful phrases? Did you write them in your notebook?

Over to you

1 Go online and read about a sport that you are not familiar with. Can you understand how the sport is practised? Would you like to try out that sport?

2 Read newspapers and magazines to find articles about what is happening in the sporting world. While it is unlikely that the exam will include a text about current sporting events, you may pick up some useful vocabulary.

3 Discuss with your friends their feelings about time based on the ideas in the text you read. Are they different from your own?

UNIT 1

Getting started

2 a

non-renewable energy resources	renewable energy resources
coal, fossil fuel, gas, peat	biofuel, biomass, ethanol, hydro-electric power, nuclear power, solar power, tidal energy, wind power

b 1 biofuel, biomass, coal, ethanol, fossil fuel, gas, peat

Spotlight on language

2 1 coal 2 oil 3 nuclear

Spotlight on exam skills 1

1 C
3 1 C 2 A 3 D

Vocabulary builder 1

1 2 conventional 3 greener 4 make up the shortfall
5 goes without saying 6 maintain our present lifestyles
7 gas-guzzling four-by-fours 8 face stark choices
9 get us out of this difficult situation
10 spend a high proportion of your income on

Spotlight on exam skills 2

1 A
2 A
3 2 ii 3 vi 4 iii 5 i 6 vii 7 iv
6 pollution, taxis, storage, cost
7 1 B 2 A 3 D
8 1 e 2 c 3 b 4 g 5 i 6 f 7 h 8 a 9 d

Vocabulary builder 2

1 1 f 2 c 3 g 4 a 5 b 6 d 7 e
3 far too (paragraph 1), too dangerous (paragraph 1), no way (paragraph 2), ever more (paragraph 3), almost certainly (paragraph 3), quite probable (paragraph 4), highly likely (paragraph 5)
4 *Suggested answers*
1 extremely 2 very; incredibly 3 totally 4 relatively
5 extremely 6 certainly

UNIT 2

Spotlight on language

1 chill out
cut down on modified starch, cut down on smoking, cut down on spirits
feel-good factor
fit as a fiddle
on cloud nine
out of condition
over the moon
sedentary lifestyle
splitting headache
stop smoking
be in high spirits
watch out, watch your weight
2 2 cut down on modified starch 3 on cloud nine /over the moon
4 chill out 5 as fit as a fiddle 6 over the moon / (on cloud nine)
7 sedentary lifestyle 8 splitting headache 9 stop smoking
10 a feel-good factor 11 watching my weight
12 out of condition

Spotlight on exam skills 1

2 1 economic output 2 the past decade 3 criticized
4 massive increases 5 sense of well-being
6 significantly gloomier 7 cultural values 8 traffic
4 **a** 1 (un)happily 2 happy 3 happy 4 happy 5 happy
6 happy 7 happily 8 (un)happily 9 happy 10 Happiness

Vocabulary builder

1 1 new-mown grass 2 City financier 3 crime statistics
4 unemployment figures 5 government policy
6 apparent paradox 7 independent body 8 labour market

Spotlight on exam skills 2

2 1 F 2 T 3 F 4 F 5 T 6 F 7 T 8 F 9 F 10 F
3 1 yes
2 not really (A metropolis is a very big city, but not every metropolis is a capital city.)
3 yes
4 not really (A boom is more specific than a change, it is a rapid increase or expansion.)
5 yes
6 no (*Overlooked* is being used metaphorically here, not literally.)
4 *Suggested answers*
1 **An advertisement** is likely to focus on visuals and have text effects like colour/bold/quotations in order to be memorable. The text is likely to be short rather than long, using the language of opinion; register is often informal to give the impression of a conversation, sometimes with imperatives. Vocabulary is likely to include positive adjectives.
A history book is likely to have long chapters, use a formal, factual style and full sentences, contain illustrations, and be organised chronologically.
2 **A legal document** is likely to be use full sentences with formal language, be very factual, contain no illustrations, use legal language with present simple tense and modal verbs and be divided into numbered sub-sections.
A newspaper article is likely to have a headline, a dramatic opening to grab attention, probably a visual, be arranged in columns with facts and quotations. Sentences may be short to be easy to understand – often sentence paragraphs. Articles don't necessarily follow chronological order, and there can be past tenses, present and future tenses.
3 **A personal story** is likely to be a balance of fact and opinion, use informal register, perhaps conversational style. It is unlikely to have headings or illustrations. Past tenses are often used to talk about something that happened.
A book review is likely to have a heading and include the language of opinion, and be short rather than long, with some sentences that summarise the key elements of the story. It is unlikely to have sections.
4 **An information leaflet** is likely to have a heading and be organised into logical sections, and makes use of visuals and short sentences for clarity. The style is factual rather than opinion-based, and is more likely to be formal than informal.
An encyclopaedia is likely to be organised alphabetically and have short factual sentences, sometimes supported by illustrations. It uses the language of explanation and definition in a relatively formal style.
5 A an encyclopaedia B a book review C a history book
D an information leaflet E a newspaper article
F an advertisement G a personal story H a legal document
6 1 B, E, G
2 A, B, E
3 B, D, E, F, G
4 E
5 C, G, H
7 1 ~~speedy~~ professional service (extract F)
2 ~~then~~ quickly followed in (extract C)
3 source of ~~considerable~~ confusion (extract B)
4 entering a ~~European~~ country (extract A)
5 ~~all~~ persons belonging to (extract H)
6 have the ~~legal~~ right to (extract D)
7 ~~university~~ degree course (extract E)
8 hardly understand ~~anything~~ (extract G)

8 1 (using) articles 2 (convicted) criminals
3 (paid) work/employment 4 relatives/family 5 naturalized
6 removal
9 *Sample answers*
1 in Paris 2 I was broke 3 spend it 4 stay at home
5 evening 6 our energy resources 7 skimming and scanning
8 immigration

UNIT 3

Getting started
1 1 drums 2 Morse code machine 3 mobile/cell/smart phone
Vocabulary builder 1
1 *Suggested answers*
business communication, channels of communication, direct communication, effective communication, effective communicator, global communication, internal communication, mass communication, non-verbal communication, online communication, poor communication, regular communication, skilled communicator, successful communication
communicate a message, communication breakdown, communicating door, communicate effectively, communicate in sign language, communication problems, communication skills, communication systems
2 2 skilled communicator
3 effective communication / communicating effectively / successful communication
4 communication skills
5 communication systems
6 regular communication
7 non-verbal communication
8 channels of communication
9 communicate in sign language
10 online communication
3 1 social media / Twitter 2 phone/landline/switchboard
3 printer/fax 4 non-verbal communication 5 Morse code
6 texting/SMS 7 letter writing
Spotlight on exam skills 1
1 1 mobile phone 2 the elite 3 (in) Nigeria 4 rural areas
5 banking (industry)
5 1 iii 2 ix 3 vii 4 viii 5 vi 6 ii
6 7 30 minutes 8 thousands of kilometres 9 (series of) clicks
10 group identity 11 factory ships 12 shipping restrictions
7 1 virtually no light (at all) 2 a fraction of a second
3 notably/particularly 4 play a role 5 set out (to) 6 collision
7 majestic 8 (seem to) point to
Spotlight on language
1 1 a, iii 2 c, ii 3 b, i
2 *Suggested answers*
1 kilogram, kilowatt 2 hydro-electric, hydrometer, hydrogen, hydrofoil 3 sub-editor, substandard, subdivision, subordinate 4 telephone, telegram, television, teleport, telecommunications, telepathic, telescope, televise 5 bipolar, biannual, biped, bicentenary, biceps, bicycle, biplane 6 post-war, postscript, postgraduate, postpone 7 pre-watershed, prefix, predestined, prefabricate, precondition, prepare, predict
Spotlight on exam skills 2
1 1 topic: overcome communication barriers
controlling idea: thinking carefully about the message
2 topic: learning foreign languages at school
controlling idea: several advantages
3 topic: publicy available computer applications
controlling idea: for obvious reasons
4 topic: new-born babies learn to become effective communicators
controlling ideas: a number of vital reasons
5 topic: learning how to get what you want in business
controlling idea: follow these steps
6 topic: starting your own blog
controlling idea: several ways to make a profit
7 topic: languages die out
controlling idea: range of different reasons
8 topic: successful advertising
controlling idea: specific features

2 1 yes 2 no 3 no 4 yes 5 yes 6 no 7 yes 8 no
4 *Suggested answers*
1 make/give 2 (holidays/Jane/etc.) 3 softly/well
4 (French/English/etc.) 5 terms (with)
6 generally/roughly/relatively 7 yourself 8 someone who
9 fluent/native 10 phone 11 part/figure
6 1 Language is one of the things that distinguishes humans from animals.
2 Latin is an example of a language that is dead but not extinct; it has no living native speakers; no children learn it from their parents; it was subject to the normal process of change in its Vulgar form; the classical form was spoken and written by the Roman upper classes.
3 Research indicates that languages are dying out at an unprecedented rate.
4 Cultural forces affect the assimilation of language.
5 Age can result in differences in speech within families and tight-knit communities.
6 Languages die out because children learn less and less of the language at home.
7 1 B 2 C 3 C 4 D 5 B
8 *Suggested underlining*
THREE
A How / functions
B software / used
C length of time / existed
D future
E Who / writes
F percentage / using
G problems
B, C, E
9 6–8 A/E/F (in any order)
Vocabulary builder 2
1 1 of 2 in 3 in 4 in 5 in 6 to 7 over/(after) 8 towards
2 1 adding information 2 time sequences 3 comparing
4 summarizing 5 giving examples 6 reporting information
7 discussing results 8 contrasting
3 1 C 2 B 3 B 4 C 5 A

UNIT 4

Getting started
2 All the ideas are good advice except *Make it clear …*; *If the interviewer makes a joke, …*; and *Be modest …*
3 1 come to nothing, come up, come clean (about something), come across as
2 do your homework, do your best, do too much
3 get results, get to the top, get on (well) with
4 give some (serious) thought to, give a (strong/confident) handshake, give a message, give yourself plenty of time
5 make sure, make a good impression, make a deliberate effort to, make it clear that, make a joke, make the mistake of, make a point of
Vocabulary builder 1
1 *Suggested answers*

require a lot of natural talent	require a lot of study/ training	likely to be in great demand in the future	not given the recognition they deserve
portrait photographer professional football player ballet dancer carpenter	chemical engineer mental-health nurse professional football player ballet dancer social worker history teacher dentist computer programmer	chemical engineer mental-health nurse social worker dentist computer programmer	chemical engineer firefighter mental-health nurse carpenter

3 1 l 2 c 3 h 4 f 5 k 6 b 7 g 8 j 9 i 10 e 11 a 12 d

4 *Suggested answers*
1 firefighter 2 dentist 3 politician / mental health worker / social worker 4 professional footballer 5 history teacher 6 carpenter 7 social worker / mental health worker 8 shopkeeper 9 ballet dancer / professional footballer 10 portrait photographer 11 chemical engineer 12 computer programmer

Spotlight on exam skills 1

1 1 In addition to banks, where do people in Switzerland invest their money? (*a location of some kind, probably a financial institution, perhaps the stock exchange*)
2 What happens to British bank accounts that are dormant for more than 15 years? (*a procedure or action: Perhaps the account is closed down and the money is given to charity, maybe the bank is allowed to keep it, maybe the government takes it.*)
3 What, according to Dr King, was the most important factor which led to the banking crisis? (*probably an event or situation: it is likely there is more than one factor involved, so you have to look for an indication that one is the most important, perhaps something about deregulation, maybe recklessness within the banks.*)
4 According to the text, who are the main instigators of banking changes in Uganda? (*probably a group of people, perhaps bankers, maybe business leaders*)
5 Which are the two most important decisions facing a couple planning to take out a mortgage? (*two factors connected to mortgages: it could be the size of the mortgage, the kind of mortgage, the length of repayment, the couple's financial circumstances*)
6 How many people in Nigeria use their mobile phone as their bank account? (*a number, perhaps expressed as a percentage: be careful of distractors of other figures and percentages around the answer.*)
7 What difficulties did the team have to overcome before they could start their business? (*a description of some problem that the group faced, perhaps something about raising capital, maybe some form filling: Distractor alert – the word before could be important, as perhaps the team also had difficulties after starting their business, but the question specifically asksfor the difficulties before.*)
8 How were small businesses in Denmark affected by the introduction of a new business tax? (information about the probably negative effects of a new tax: *As with item 7, the word* following *could be important. There could be some information about the way the business were affected before the tax was introduced as a distractor.*)

3 1 a) a verb b) negative – C
2 a) a noun b) negative – B
3 speaking – B
4 a) idiomatic b) negative – A
5 a) action b) negative – A
6 a) quality b) negative – D

4 1 D 2 C 3 A

Vocabulary builder 2

1 1 g 2 j 3 m 4 b 5 a 6 c 7 s 8 p 9 e 10 n 11 k 12 d 13 h 14 q 15 l 16 f 17 r 18 o 19 i

2 1 prosperous 2 entrepreneur 4 erroneous 7 traditionally 9 finding 10 roots 11 to a certain extent 12 view 13 carried out 14 frequently 15 multiple 16 trait 17 crucial 18 set up 19 explains

3 1 yes 2 yes 3 no 4 yes 5 no 6 yes 7 no 8 no 9 yes 10 yes

4 1 job losses 2 doing well 3 for the best 4 struggling 5 proliferation 6 entrepreneurs 7 redundancy cheque

5 *Suggested answers*
1 People can benefit from losing a job if they are actually future entrepreneurs.
2 Many people start up their own small business using redundancy cheques on losing their jobs in difficult economic conditions.
3 Tough trading conditions can cause businesses to suffer, but can also result in the creation of new businesses.

Spotlight on exam skills 2

1 A Money in all its forms B Currencies and copies C The cost of cash D The future is here

2 1 A 2 D 3 E 4 A 5 C 6 E 7 B 8 E

3 1 cashless 2 counterfeiting 3 banking infrastructure 4 exchange offices

8 1 H 2 D 3 B 4 A 5 F 6 C 7 B 8 F 9 K 10 C 11 L 12 E 13 J 14 N

UNIT 5

Getting started

1 *Suggested answers*
1 d, e 2 b 3 i 4 a 5 h, k 6 l 7 f, g 8 b, c, j 9 e

3 1 law-abiding citizen 2 live within your means 3 be out of work 4 no one to turn to 5 drop out 6 freedom of the press

Vocabulary builder

1 *Suggested answers*
labour rates, sexual violence, sexual orientation, sexual crime, sexual discrimination, sexual abuse, sexual crimes, illegal immigrants, underage pregnancy, child pregnancy, social issues, social unrest, animal abuse, ethnic minorities, ethnic groups, teenage pregnancy, drug abuse, civilized society, domestic violence, ethnic minority, child abuse, child labour, minority rights, crime rates, animal rights, hate crimes

Spotlight on exam skills 1

1 2 teenage/underage pregnancy 3 crime rates 4 drug abuse 5 civilized society 6 sexual discrimination 7 sexual orientation 8 child labour 9 domestic violence 10 ethnic minorities 11 illegal immigrants 12 animal rights 13 hate crimes 14 minority groups 15 social unrest

2 *Suggested answers*
1 While it is impossible to attribute this to one single cause, it is often pointed out that [...] is a frequent motive for crime ...
2 What's more, it almost guarantees that they will be unable to finish their education, and in all likelihood, that will have severe consequences for the sort of work they will be able to find, if any.
3 The end of [...] in the workplace means that women are no longer paid less than men for the same job.
4 These are positive steps.
5 People are insulted, attacked or worse for being black, or gay, or followers of a different religion.
6 They tend to work hard, often doing the jobs we consider beneath us.
7 Civil disturbance, the breakdown of law and order ...
8 Ask any members of a [...] and they will tell you they know someone who has experienced this personally, and that it makes them feel like second-class citizens.

3 general point—specific details: Text C
statement—qualification of the statement: Text D
opinion—support for the opinion: Text F
question—answer: Text G
problem—solution: Text B

6 1 C, D 2 A 3 B 4 C 5 B 6 E 7 widespread co-operation 8 expected 9 organizations and systems 10 cheating

Spotlight on language

1 1 a 2 a 3 b 4 a 5 a 6 c 7 b 8 a 9 c 10 a

2 1 both 2 both 3 to be changed 4 to be said 5 to be suggesting 6 to be seen 7 to be improving 8 to put 9 to be appreciated; be considered 10 to be taking

Spotlight on exam skills 2

1 undesirable 2 (relatively) trivial 3 murder 4 influence 5 drug abuse 6 Native Americans 7 sharp rise 8 Mass media 9 worse 10 stereotypes 11 reinforced 12 success 13 C 14 G 15 E 16 A

UNIT 6

Getting started

1 a *Suggested answers*
1 e 2 c, d 3 a, e, g 4 c, j 5 e, i 6 b, f 7 a, c 8 e, f 9 h
b See above.

3 a smog; unleaded petrol
b endangered species; loss of habitat
c pesticides and chemical compounds
d drinkable water; contamination of rivers, lakes and seas; risk of disease
e floods and droughts; polar ice caps
f illegal logging and cutting down the rainforest
g safe and renewable energy; the consumer society
h overfishing; fleet of trawlers
i acid rain; ultraviolet
j rubbish dumps; recycling; landfill

Spotlight on exam skills 1

1 1 e 2 g 3 d 4 b 5 c 6 a 7 j 8 i 9 h 10 f
2 1 filtered (out) 2 skin cancer 3 gradual improvement 4 acid rain 5 (chronic) respiratory illnesses 6 factories 7 hormone balance 8 unleaded petrol 9 the sea / the ocean 10 mass extinction 11 poorer countries 12 farmers

Vocabulary builder

1 1 converted 2 translated 3 transformed 4 distorted 5 merge 6 deteriorated 7 adjust 8 renovated 9 emigrated 10 transferred 11 escalate 12 adapt
3 1 remove 2 transform 3 reinforce 4 disguise 5 embellish
4 *Suggested answers*
1 ruined 2 expanded/grew/transformed 3 rejuvenated 4 rein in 5 damage/ruin 6 ruin/shape/transform 7 risen/rocketed/soared 8 embellish/disguise
6 1 purification 2 colonize 3 classified 4 justify 5 justified 6 homogenized/homogenous 7 hospitalize 8 minimum 9 clarification 10 automated/automatic 11 simplicity 12 computerize/compute 13 computerized
7 1 purification/homogenization 2 computerized/automated 3 justification 4 clarify 5 colony 6 simplified 7 classification 8 minimal

Spotlight on exam skills 2

1 (holding) basin 2 particle filter 3 chlorine 4 high pressure 5 (Dissolved) Salts 6 source / the sea 7 blending
8/9/10 A, C, D (in any order)

Spotlight on language

1 1 **a** if we want to
b if we didn't use them / if that were not the case
c If exploitation
2 **a** Unless something **b** as long as **c** whether or not
3 **a** if the situation is to change **b** if you are poor
c If that were not the case
4 **a** If we look back **b** otherwise **c** If we continue
2 1 c) is different, as the others focus on man's need or right to exploit resources, not on the consequences for the planet.
2 All three are similar.
3 a) is different, as it does not focus on the reason for child labour.
4 b) is the only one that implies today's change is not natural.
3 *Sample answers*
1 As long as I work hard, I should do well in the exam.
2 Having a good level of English is important, otherwise it's hard to get a good job in my country.
3 I want to get a good result in my IELTS exam. If that were not the case, I wouldn't be studying so hard.
4 My plans for the future depend on whether or not I go to university.
5 If I continue to develop my vocabulary and practise, I'll be able to read faster and understand more.
6 If I look back on the past year, the things that have been most important for me include deciding to study for IELTS and saving for a great holiday abroad.
7 Unless something unexpected happens, I will probably go to university abroad soon.
8 If people like me want to make a big difference to the world, we have to remember that actions speak louder than words.
9 I think if people want to tackle the problems of the environment, we have to make a conscious decision to consume less of everything.
10 If I want to fulfil my ambitions and make my dreams come true, I will have to work hard.

5 1 if at all / if anything 2 if I were you
3 If it's all the same to you / If you don't mind
4 If anything / If you ask me 5 If it comes to that 6 If only
7 if necessary / if it comes/came to that 8 So what if

Spotlight on exam skills 3

1 1 oxygen 2 fermentation 3 biogas 4 enzymes 5 toxic chemicals 6 xerophiles 7 absorb 8 vinegar

UNIT 7

Getting started

2 *Suggested answers*

electric toothbrush	hybrid car	milk
time-saving healthy gums long-lasting smile labour-saving for whiter teeth	low cost precision-engineered money-saving high performance environmental impact	high in protein great taste low-fat good for you

Vocabulary builder 1

1 1 F 2 T 3 NG 4 T 5 NG 6 T 7 F 8 F 9 F
2 *Suggested answers*
advertising watchdog, advertising claims, telemarketing, spam email, print advertising, outdoor advertising
3 2 sales revenue, g 3 product launch, a 4 exclusive rights, b 5 good reputation, d 6 market research, h 7 brand loyalty, e 8 franchise agreement, f 9 celebrity endorsement, i

Spotlight on exam skills 1

1 F 2 NG 3 NG 4 T 5 T 6 T 7 F 8 T

Vocabulary builder 2

1 1 ego 2 affluent 3 eye-catching 4 addiction 5 lifestyle
2 shopaholic
3 1 mail 2 through 3 proportions 4 material 5 come by 6 closely 7 environmental 8 sheer 9 developed 10 in it
4 1 to 2 for 3 on 4 in

Spotlight on exam skills 2

2 1 F 2 T 3 F 4 NG 5 T 6 F 7 NG 8 T
3 1 NG 2 T 3 F 4 NG 5 F
4 *Sample answers*
1 This is something that has improved considerably. / X has got a lot better / has changed for the better / is much better.
2 In those days, everybody did the same. / This was the norm then. / This was what people did then.
3 make decisions based on what they had read / let what they had heard or seen influence their choices
4 With the years / In the course of time / Over the years / With the passage of time
5 (Quite) soon / Before long / In only a matter of (days/weeks/months)

Spotlight on language

1 1 **process** = series of stages needed to perform an operation of some sort
procedure = the agreed correct way of doing something
production line = the line of machines/workers that produces a manufactured product
2 **job** = **1** a particular thing you have to do; **2** work for which you get paid
career = the series of jobs a person has over time, often in one field, often progressively more important
profession = a type of job that needs particular training and qualifications
business = **1** a commercial organisation; **2** the activity of trading for money; **3** work that is part of your job
3 **launch your product** = to begin the promotion of a new product
promote your product = to do any of the activities that bring your product to public attention
stock your product = when a seller regularly keeps examples of your product to sell

4 **sell by** = 1 how you sell something; 2 the date by which something (normally food) must be sold before for health reasons
sell out = every example of the product has been sold
sell for = the price of a product or service
5 **earn something** = 1 to get money for what you do; 2 to get something (like a chance to relax or a good reputation) in return for your efforts, normally positive
deserve something = you have the right to something because of your hard work
be worth something = to have a certain value
6 **man management** = the specific techniques that are the way you manage people
middle management = the people who have responsibilities for managing groups of people in a company, but who are not at the top of company taking the most important decisions
micro management = normally seen as a negative style of managing people with tight control over every detail of the job
7 **acknowledge** = 1 to accept that something is true; 2 to say you have received business correspondence; 3 to publicly express thanks to someone for help received
admit = to agree something – often negative – has happened.
agree = 1 to have the same opinion as someone; 2 to say 'yes' to something
8 **claim** = 1 to report what someone says, without indicating if you agree or not; 2 to say something is true, although this has not been proved for sure
state = to formally and often officially say something
allege = to state something is true, but without giving proof of this

2 1 procedure; process 2 career; business 3 promote your product; stock your product 4 sell-by; sell out 5 deserve; earn 6 middle management; micro-management 7 agree; acknowledge 8 claim; allege

3 *Sample answers*
1 ... many companies have workers who operate in shifts 24 hours a day.
2 ... nowadays is software design.
3 ... there is so much competition, and you can never be sure how the public will react to something new.
4 ... thousands of pounds/dollars/euros.
5 ... is an important skill and is essential if you want to be successful.

Spotlight on exam skills 3

1 1 TRUE 2 NOT GIVEN 3 TRUE 4 NOT GIVEN 5 FALSE 6 brief 7 an analysis 8 range of factors 9 cost-effective 10 brand awareness 11 within budget 12 measure of success

2 a 1 loathe 2 goes 3 vast 4 around 5 share 6 number 7 key

UNIT 8

Spotlight on exam skills 1

1 No (... *not given to everyone.*)
2 Yes (*application/training/long hours*)
3 Not Given
4 Yes (... *turn their backs on the parties and socialising of their peers* ...)
5 Not Given
6 True (... *something that is all too often overlooked* ...)

Vocabulary builder

1

positive	negative
to meet your objectives to make a dream come true to fall on your feet to achieve your full potential to go from strength to strength to fulfil an ambition to hit the jackpot to go according to plan	to go unrecognized to fall at the last hurdle to backfire to come to nothing to not cut the mustard to bomb to go down the drain to fall by the wayside to go belly up to leave something to be desired

2 1 fulfil their ambition / make their dream come true
2 go unrecognized
3 cut the mustard
4 hit the jackpot
5 went belly up / came to nothing / went down the drain / bombed / fell by the wayside

4 *Suggested answers*
highly valued; to do badly (in exams); good exam results; winning (part of the race); well-rewarded; (local, national or international) acclaim; financial rewards; achievements

6 1 succeed 2 Failure 3 failure; failure 4 successful 5 fail 6 failure 7 fail; failure 8 failure 9 successful 10 failure

7

	does not collocate	completes the sentence
1	make a failure	make a deal
2	hit the success	hit rock bottom
3	lose an idea	lost a fortune
4	gain practice	gaining ground
5	win some decisions	win hands down
6	deserve failure	deserve a medal / deserve a holiday / deserve a mention
7	earn your car	earn a reputation

Spotlight on language

1 2 negative: *uncertain*; distractor: *excellent reputation*
3 neutral
4 negative: *spectacular decline, no light at the end of the tunnel*
5 neutral
6 positive: *the benefits it brings ... far outweigh the negative aspects*; distractors: *pollution, accidents*
7 negative: *facing bankruptcy*; distractor: *a promising start*
8 negative: *only reason*; distractors: *fulfilment, personal satisfaction*

2 1 g 2 e 3 d 4 a 5 f 6 c 7 b

3 1 stating a fact
2 It implies that he is original and perhaps a little crazy.
3 somewhere between neutral and negative: It makes him sound a little greedy.
4 positive
5 positive
6 negative
7 *An unqualified disaster* is much stronger – and very negative.
8 unimpressed, disappointed, unnecessarily negative
9 plunged, went down, plummeted, declined rapidly, fell like a stone
10 went into administration, went bankrupt, ceased trading, closed its doors

Spotlight on exam skills 2

1 1 c 2 a 3 f 4 b 5 d 6 e

3 1 YES 2 NO 3 NOT GIVEN 4 YES 5 NO 6 neglect 7 (being) driven 8 obese 9 fitness levels 10 B 11 C 12 E 13 A 14 v 15 iii 16 i 17 viii 18 vi 19 ix 20 FALSE 21 TRUE 22 NOT GIVEN 23 TRUE 24 D 25 B 26 B 27 C

UNIT 9

Getting started

3 1 B 2 A 3 A 4 B 5 C 6 A 7 A 8 C 9 B 10 C 11 B 12 A

4 1 l 2 f 3 c 4 g 5 d 6 e 7 k 8 j 9 b 10 i 11 a 12 h

5

quantity	time
a minimum of fuss in great numbers great flocks the air is filled with ... stacks of them all over the floor a host of reasons a pack of lies swarms a thousand angry individuals in great (multicoloured) heaps the throng	after spending some time ... It's the time of year when ... weeks of practice (unread) for years (took) the best part of a day from start to finish in autumn

movement	relating to behaviour
a long migration across (the plains) moved off into the distance descend on (hear something) coming your way (watching as) they came into view push through (the throng)	springs into action put behind bars treat them with respect

Spotlight on language 1

2 i 3 e 4 f 5 h 6 a 7 b 8 j 9 g 10 d

Spotlight on exam skills 1

1 E 2 D 3 F 4 A 5 G 6 C 7 B
8 D 9 B 10 D 11 A 12 C
13 B

Vocabulary builder

1 1 b 2 b 3 a 4 b 5 b 6 b 7 a 8 b 9 b 10 a 11 b 12 b
2 1 perspective 2 loose 3 drawbacks 4 in-laws 5 Primates

Spotlight on language 2

1 2 (paragraph E), 3 (paragraph G), 4 (paragraph A), 7 (paragraph D), 9 (paragraph F), 10 (paragraph B), 11 (paragraph C)

2

concentrating on difference	concentrating on similarity
unlike, in contrast, tell the difference, distinguish between, tell apart, by contrast, differ in many respects, there's no comparison, huge contrast, discrepancy between, unique	similar, identical, akin, alike, likewise, have a lot in common, (bear) a resemblance, look the same, similarly, a striking similarity, in the same vein, share an opinion, follow someone's lead

3
1 similar / identical / alike / the same; distinguish between / tell the difference between
2 a resemblance / a striking similarity
3 discrepancy between
4 unlike
5 have a lot in common
6 unlike
7 unique; identical / the same; tell apart
8 akin; likewise / the same
9 in the same vein
10 follow its lead

4 *Sample answers*
1 My country has a lot in common with the USA in terms of the popularity of cars as a means of transport.
2 The way I was educated differs in many respects from what school was like in my grandparents' time.
3 The problems my generation faces today are unlike those previous generations worried about.
4 In my opinion, there's a huge contrast between the priorities of rich and poor countries.
5 Unlike when I was growing up, nowadays even the youngest children have mobile phones and computers.

Spotlight on exam skills 2

14 D 15 C 16 A 17 B
18–20 A, B, F (in any order)
21 I 22 L 23 J 24 F 25 C 26 E

UNIT 10

Getting started

3 1 in 2 of 3 off 4 for 5 up 6 of 7 in 8 out 9 in 10 by 11 for 12 of 13 against 14 on 15 against
4 1 a 2 c 3 b 4 a 5 e (skiing) 6 b 7 d 8 e (table tennis / ping-pong) 9 c 10 d 11 a 12 c

Spotlight on exam skills 1

1 1 (three) plum trees 2 women's changing rooms 3 shower(s) 4 equipment room 5 main sports hall 6 first(-)aid room
2 C
3 1 vi 2 iv 3 i
4 1 spelling mistakes 2 maximum 3 (test) format
5 1 Read the rubric. 2 (from) the passage
6 *Sample answers*
1 What's in the corner of the changing rooms?
2 Who can use the crèche? / Who's the crèche for?
3 What's opposite the equipment storage room?
4 Who helps with accidents? / Do you have anyone who can help with injuries?

Spotlight on language

1 1 they first met 2 they had graduated 3 we got home 4 on completing 5 you have lived abroad 6 the manager had spoken 7 the invention of the telescope 8 modern computers 9 She had a successful career 10 a colder-than-expected winter 11 previous setbacks 12 to examine 13 a technical problem 14 Trials of the new drug
2 1 b 2 b 3 a 4 a 5 b 6 a 7 b 8 a 9 b 10 a 11 a 12 b 13 b 14 a 15 a

Spotlight on exam skills 2

1 H 2 E 3 B 4 A 5 C 6 D
7 G 8 D 9 I 10 B 11 H 12 F
13 C

Answer-sheet skills (page 140)

a the candidate number in the boxes
b everywhere!
c question 23
d question 9 (You are generally asked for one, two or three words as a maximum.)
e question 29
f Are you male/female?
g module taken
h question 34
i question 7 (Answer should be *hospital*.)
j the name
k questions 11, 24
l questions 12–16
m question 14
n questions 20–21
o question 38

Dictionary skills (page 143)

1 1 formal: thereby, expurgate, upon, ascertain, inadvisable, superannuated
informal: thingummy, meanie, scuzzy, jeepers, upchuck, hurt like crazy, chill out, up for grabs, stonking
2 British English: naff, spanner, bonnet, barrister, crisps, practise
American English: sidewalk, Monday through Friday, third grade, parking lot, thumbtack, oftentimes, elevator
3 countable nouns: account, eclipse, crumb
uncountable nouns: luggage, information, toast, news, fast food, ebony
4 current expressions: netizen, geek
old-fashioned expressions: by jingo, twerp, a rum do, poltroon, blithering, stone me!, super-duper
2 medical terms: asthma, anaemic, benign, chickenpox, dehydrated, inflamed, seizure
plants and flowers: violet, stamen, pollen, biennial, deciduous
3 1 hard 2 chance 3 then/again 4 mountain 5 none 6 mind 7 come 8 drop

Useful websites for IELTS reading practice

The reading passages in the IELTS test are designed to be suitably academic to help you practise the skills needed by university students. Therefore, while all reading is good, not all websites will be equally useful as preparation for the exam. The list below is far from exhaustive, but it does focus on the sort of websites that can be sources for the reading passages.

BBC News	www.bbc.co.uk/news
The Guardian	www.guardian.co.uk
The Economist	www.economist.com
New Scientist	www.newscientist.com
Scientific American	www.scientificamerican.com
American Scientist	www.americanscientist.org
National Geographic	www.nationalgeographic.com
Washington Post	www.washingtonpost.com
Sydney Morning Herald	www.smh.com.au
Wall Street Journal	wsj.com/home-page
Nature	www.nature.com/
Forbes	www.forbes.com/
Harvard Business Review	hbr.org
Conservation	www.conservationmagazine.org
Science Daily	www.sciencedaily.com
Management Today	www.managementtoday.co.uk
Scientific American Mind	www.scientificamerican.com/sciammind
History Today	www.historytoday.com/

There are hundreds of websites about IELTS, and the quality is very variable, so be careful. The key IELTS website to check is www.ielts.org.

You'll also find useful information on the British Council website: www.britishcouncil.org/learning-ielts.htm

All URLs are correct at time of going to press, but the authors and publisher can accept no responsibility for their subsequent content or accuracy.

My own list of useful websites for IELTS Reading Paper practice

name of site	web address

How this book will help you with the other IELTS papers

Being a good reader is a key skill in life, and is essential for students at university. In fact, studies indicate that there is a strong link between reading a lot and academic success. Most of us would admit that the people we know who write best and speak more fluently and impressively are also the people who read widely and frequently. That's another reason why getting into the habit of regularly reading a range of English texts is a great basis for increasing your language skills in general.

Reading isn't just about understanding words, as you have seen in this book. Reading is about understanding how sentences and paragraphs are structured to present ideas as effectively as possible. It is about knowing how writers are structuring texts, making an argument, supporting their points and trying to influence the reader. Good readers are people who know how language is used to communicate effectively.

How can this book help you with the Speaking Paper?

Firstly, by reading extensively, you will become familiar with a range of interesting topics. This means you will have more to say about more things. You will know different people's opinions on a variety of topics from ecology to technology, medicine to educational standards, economic issues to threats and challenges facing us now and shaping our future. Being familiar with other people's thoughts and opinions on these topics can help you express your own opinions on them. Knowing what different groups of people in the English-speaking world think about a topic means you have the ability to compare and contrast the situation in your country. This gives you a better balanced, more informed and more interesting view. You will be able to talk about your views, and compare them to the views and opinions of the authors you have read.

In addition, when you state your views and opinions, you can refer to what you have read, where and when you read it. This helps you contextualize your views, and it shows you are a regular reader and open to new ideas – which could impress the examiner. It also gives you more to say, using expressions like the following:

Well, according to an article I was reading in a British magazine the other day, ...

I know from the reading I have done that many people believe / are worried about / would like to ...

As the papers say, ...

It's difficult to open a newspaper these days without finding a story about ...

In addition, reading is a great way of developing your vocabulary and grammar. When you read, you see how ideas are linked by expressions such as *on the other hand, nevertheless, for a start, initially, as far as I am aware, however, even though*. These are the building blocks of arguments and discussion. You will notice which are most frequent, and these are the ones you should try to use more frequently in your own speaking.

How can this book help you with the Writing Paper?

We have already seen that most good writers are also frequent readers. But there is more to it than that. There is a connection between reading a lot and spelling better and having a more developed vocabulary.

When you read, you notice that ideas can be expressed in a variety of different ways. Sentences can be linked in different ways. Sometimes it is even necessary to 'read between the lines' to find the author's opinion. In other words, you can learn about style and structure by reading. You will know how to structure an introduction. You will see different techniques for underlining your points. You will see that good writers avoid repetition of words and phrases because it becomes boring for the reader. You will learn how to use synonyms and paraphrase techniques to achieve your effect.

Again, when you write in IELTS, it is often useful and good academic style to justify the points you are making by using examples. When you read a lot, you can do this by referring to what you have read.

How can this book help you with the Listening Paper?

Firstly, of course, the listening could well be on topics that you have read about. In fact, the more you read, the more likely it is that you will be familiar with some element of the topic of the listening. And while the questions in the listening will never test your general knowledge, it is a definite advantage if you are on familiar ground. For a start, you are more likely to know some of the key words and expressions on the topic, so there will be less that is absolutely new to you. That will help your confidence.

In addition, reading longer texts is good practice for improving your attention span when listening to longer recordings. What's more, the more formal and academic listenings are sometimes texts that are written to be read, and they have a lot in common with reading texts. You will hear many of the same structuring expressions, you will recognize introductions and conclusions. You will be able to distinguish between a fact and an opinion.

What worries many students about the Listening Paper is that the speakers will speak quickly, and that there will be new words and expressions that could prove confusing. If you are used to dealing with new words and expressions in reading texts, that will be less of a problem. And your reading practice will have helped you increase your vocabulary.

Another advantage concerns your memory. Reading improves your memory; the Listening Paper makes demands on your short-term memory, as you only hear the text once. So people used to reading longer texts tend to be better able to remember the contents of listening better, too.

Vocabulary skills

Good readers have a good vocabulary. In your own language, there is a difference between your productive, or 'active', vocabulary and your receptive, or 'passive', vocabulary. Your productive vocabulary includes all the words and expressions that you can use accurately and appropriately. This is very important in the Speaking and Writing Papers. Your receptive vocabulary is larger than your productive vocabulary and includes all the words and expressions that you recognize or can understand in context, but which you do not make active use of when speaking or writing. You are probably able to process a large number of words and expressions on technical and semi-technical topics that you do not feel comfortable about using in your productive vocabulary.

Being able to decide whether it is worth learning a word or expression is a key decision you have to make. Students can waste a lot of time looking up, recording and trying to learn items that are really best considered part of their passive vocabulary.

Here are eight key skills in developing an extensive vocabulary:

1 When you see a new word or phrase, decide if you think it is useful for you or not. Don't try to learn and use all new items, as these are sure to include words that you don't and won't need in your everyday life. This saves you time and allows you to focus on developing your productive or 'active' vocabulary.

2 Read extensively. If you only read articles from one source on one topic, you are limiting yourself. Besides, the Reading passages in the IELTS test will come from a variety of different sources. Read newspapers, magazines, journals, professional publications, literature, technical leaflets and more – the more you read, the better. By reading more, you become familiar with different styles, different formats, different topics and the vocabulary of those topics. If you read widely and notice some key words occurring in texts on different topics, they are likely to be very important and useful words.

3 When you come across a new word, always look at the context it is in. When you record a new word, add information about the context. For example, the word *table* seems easy enough: it's a piece of furniture you eat off in the kitchen or dining room. But in business, you can *table a motion*; at school, you learn your *two-times table*; books have a *table of contents*; and a sports team that is *top of the table* is doing well in a league or competition. In other words, the meaning of a word or expression depends very much on the context it is used in.

4 Learn some key 'word-attack' skills. These are the skills that help you work out what a new word might mean. For example, decide which of these invented words is a noun, verb or adjective, then check your answers at the bottom of page 139:
hibletiness, broughtious, scrindled, unpreduntlitude, magnistific
You probably looked at the beginnings and endings of the words to help you decide. Likewise, word-attack skills will help you guess whether a word is positive or negative, real or invented, modern or archaic.

5 When you look up a new word or expression, make sure you have a system for recording it if you decide it is worth learning. You should not just focus on the meaning or translation into your language. At IELTS level, words and expressions do not all have direct translatable equivalents. You should record the context it occurs in, and any details to help you pronounce it correctly, such as the transcription using IPA symbols and the stress pattern. You also need to know the grammar patterns associated with the word – and whether it is irregular in any form.

6 If you decide a word or expression is worth learning, then you should also plan to use it yourself. Don't just leave it in your notebook; use it in your next essay. Plan to have a conversation on the topic so you can use it. You will need to use a new language item several times before it sticks in your memory.

7 Don't learn words in isolation. Learn combinations: learn a noun with an adjective that goes with it; learn a verb with a suitable adverb. For example, when you look up the word *decide*, you could learn these combinations:
make a decision
decide (not) to do something
a difficult decision
decide on a course of action
decide in someone's favour
decide whether
still haven't decided
decide what to do
reach a decision
the moment of decision
be decisive

8 When you decide to learn a new word, also learn the positive and negative forms, the opposites, any fixed expressions the word occurs in, and, if relevant, learn related terms. For example, if you learn the word *daily*, you can guess the words *hourly, weekly, monthly, yearly* – but careful: *minutely* has a different and unrelated meaning, and *decadely* and *centurily* do not exist.
If you learn *meaningful*, then also check for *meaningless, unmeaningful, meaningfully, meaninglessness*, etc.

Key
hibletiness, unpredauntlitude: noun forms
broughtious, magnistific: adjective forms
scrindled: verb form

Answer-sheet skills

1 Look at the completed answer sheet on page 141. Can you find at least ten mistakes?

2 Match these errors to the answer sheet.

- **a** This number is wrong.
- **b** You should write in pencil.
- **c** Use roman numerals for these answers.
- **d** Too many words – check the limit.
- **e** Check your grammar for accuracy.
- **f** Don't tick – shade the box.
- **g** Remember to indicate which exam you are taking.
- **h** This is not one of the possible answers for this question.
- **i** Check your spelling carefully.
- **j** This should be in CAPITALS.
- **k** Don't leave any answers blank.
- **l** Remember, there will be at least one example of each option with True / False / Not Given questions.
- **m** Follow the rubric – don't use abbreviations.
- **n** The same phrase will not be the answer to more than one question.
- **o** Choose just one answer.

3 Guidelines for completing the answer sheet correctly.

1. Read the instructions to each question carefully and follow them.
2. Look at any examples given and make sure you understand them.
3. Read the instructions on the answer sheet carefully and follow them.
4. If you make a mistake, just cross it out with a single line and write your answer next to it.
5. Copy your answers carefully when you are completing the answer sheet.
6. Check your spelling.
7. Check your grammar (especially singular/plural; present/past; positive/negative).
8. Copy your answers section by section. Don't try to copy all the answers in one go.
9. Make sure you leave no blanks.
10. Leave yourself sufficient time to copy the answers and to check them.

Please write your **full name** in CAPITAL letters on the line below:

Mohammed Almasi

Please write your Candidate number on the line below:

276

Please write your three digit language code in the boxes and shade the numbers in the grid on the right.

0	1	2	3	4	5	6	7	8	9
0	1	2	3	4	5	6	7	8	9
0	1	2	3	4	5	6	7	8	9

Are you: Female? ▭ Male? ✓

Reading Reading Reading Reading Reading Reading

Module taken (shade one box): Academic ▭ General Training ▭

		Marker use only			Marker use only
1	A	✓ 1 ✗	**21**	build on	✓ 21 ✗
2	D	✓ 2 ✗	**22**	vi	✓ 22 ✗
3	E	✓ 3 ✗	**23**	4	✓ 23 ✗
4	B	✓ 4 ✗	**24**		✓ 24 ✗
5	G	✓ 5 ✗	**25**	viii	✓ 25 ✗
6	C	✓ 6 ✗	**26**	ix	✓ 26 ✗
7	hosispital	✓ 7 ✗	**27**	no fixed pattern	✓ 27 ✗
8	patients and nurses	✓ 8 ✗	**28**	~~sufficient evidence~~ general advice	✓ 28 ✗
9	for at least two or more weeks	✓ 9 ✗	**29**	not much people	✓ 29 ✗
10	an operation	✓ 10 ✗	**30**	useful explanations	✓ 30 ✗
11		✓ 11 ✗	**31**	yes	✓ 31 ✗
12	True	✓ 12 ✗	**32**	yes	✓ 32 ✗
13	False	✓ 13 ✗	**33**	not given	✓ 33 ✗
14	T	✓ 14 ✗	**34**	not	✓ 34 ✗
15	False	✓ 15 ✗	**35**	no	✓ 35 ✗
16	True	✓ 16 ✗	**36**	B	✓ 36 ✗
17	basis	✓ 17 ✗	**37**	E	✓ 37 ✗
18	training	✓ 18 ✗	**38**	A or B	✓ 38 ✗
19	access	✓ 19 ✗	**39**	D	✓ 39 ✗
20	build on	✓ 20 ✗	**40**	C	✓ 40 ✗

Marker 2 Initials		Marker 1 Initials		Band Score		Reading Total	

Dictionary skills

To give yourself the best chance of getting a good result in IELTS, you need to have a good English–English dictionary. This will also help you when you are living, working and studying in an English-speaking country.

Which of these features does your dictionary have?

1 over 120,000 words and expressions
2 clear explanations and definitions using easy language
3 examples of the word or expression in context
4 phonetic transcriptions of each word to help you pronounce words you have not heard before
5 grammar information, such as part of speech
6 information about alternative spellings or pronounciation
7 details of irregular forms
8 details about whether words are, for example, British or American English
9 details about whether words are humorous, rude, informal, formal, etc.
10 grammar information about the verb patterns for all verbs
11 information about how common/useful key words and expressions are
12 idiomatic expressions
13 information about related words, opposites and synonyms
14 a CD-ROM with audio
15 an introduction which explains the contents and organization of the dictionary, including the meaning of all codes and abbreviations

The three most common student problems with dictionaries

1 **Overusing a dictionary**
Don't stop reading and look up every new word in a dictionary. That can make you 'dictionary dependent'. It's good to try to work out what a new word means from the context. It also saves time if you decide to read on and only look up those words that appear to be essential to the meaning of the text. Remember, not all words are worth learning – some are so technical that you are unlikely to ever use them. Also, you will not be allowed to use a dictionary in the IELTS test, so it is a good idea to give yourself lots of practice reading texts without looking up new words.

2 **Underusing a dictionary**
Dictionaries today contain a wealth of useful information about words and expressions. When you look up a word, you can learn not just the meaning, but also the grammar patterns it occurs in, the forms it combines with, when to use it – or not use it. Dictionaries can help you distinguish between confusing terms such as *raise/rise, earn/deserve, make/do, economical/economic* and many more. This means that if you know how to use a dictionary well, you can look up one word and learn much more than one thing, as you can learn what the word means, expressions it occurs in, related terms, and how to use it in different contexts.

3 **Using a dictionary but not understanding all the information in it**
It is important for you to be able to understand the grammar codes and the IPA symbols so you can pronounce a new word properly and use it accurately and appropriately in your writing.

Dictionary practice

1 Use your dictionary to find which of the two categories each of these words and expressions belongs to.

1 **formal/informal**

thingummy thereby meanie scuzzy expurgate jeepers upon upchuck hurt like crazy chill out ascertain inadvisable up for grabs stonking superannuated

2 **British/American English**

sidewalk Monday through Friday naff third grade parking lot spanner bonnet barrister crisps thumbtack oftentimes elevator practise

3 **countable/uncountable nouns**

luggage information toast news account fast food ebony eclipse crumb

4 **current/old-fashioned expressions**

by jingo twerp a rum do netizen poltroon blithering geek stone me! super-duper

2 Divide these words into two categories: 'medical terms' and 'plants and flowers'.

asthma violet anaemic benign stamen pollen chickenpox biennial dehydrated inflamed deciduous seizure

3 Use your dictionary to find the missing word in these phrases and expressions.

1 by dint of .... work
2 to have a fighting ....
3 every now and ....
4 make a .... out of a molehill
5 second to ....
6 it crossed my ....
7 take things as they ....
8 at the .... of a hat

A summary of IELTS tips

1. Read, read, read. Get into the habit of reading something every day, and read widely. Start doing this several months before the date of your test.
2. Practise skimming and scanning. You should read each text quickly before you start to look for the answers so you know what it is about in general, what type of text it is, and what information is where.
3. Develop your vocabulary.
4. Look for the topic sentence in each paragraph.
5. Don't worry about words or phrases you don't know. They might not be important.
6. Be strict about managing your time in the exam: 20 minutes per passage, including time to fill in the answer sheet.
7. Make sure you identify the key words in each question, paying attention to words like *often, must, some, before*.
8. Never leave a blank on the answer sheet.
9. Check you know how many words are required in your answers and stick to the limit. Don't use unnecessary words.
10. Look for synonyms and paraphrases in the question and the reading passage.
11. Be careful with distractors. Often if you find the same word in a question and in the passage, it will be part of a wrong answer.
12. Check you know what is required for the different task types.
13. Double-check your spelling.
14. Remember that in most task types, the questions generally follow in order through the text.
15. Don't spend too long on one question. If it is too difficult, move on to the next one.
16. Fill in the answers to the questions on each reading passage when you have finished that section. This will help avoid problems of putting the answer in the wrong place.
17. Underline key information that gives you an answer in the reading passage.
18. Look at any sample answers to check you understand the task and type of answer required.
19. Remember that there will be at least one of each answer with True / False / Not Given or Yes / No / Not Given questions.
20. Get a good dictionary, learn how to use it properly and learn some useful words and expressions every day.

Good luck in the IELTS test!